IT HAPPENED IN
PHILADELPHIA

Scott Bruce

WITHDRAWN

TWODOT®

GUILFORD, CONNECTICUT
HELENA, MONTANA
AN IMPRINT OF THE GLOBE PEQUOT PRESS

A · T W O D O T® · B O O K

Copyright © 2008 Morris Book Publishing, LLC

Text design by Nancy Freeborn

Map by Daniel Lloyd © 2008 Morris Book Publishing, LLC

Library of Congress Cataloging-in-Publication Data is available on file.

ISBN 978-0-7627-3989-9

Printed in the United States of America

10 9 8 7 6 5 4 3 2 1

This book is dedicated to
my heart, my partner, my love, my wife . . . Anne.

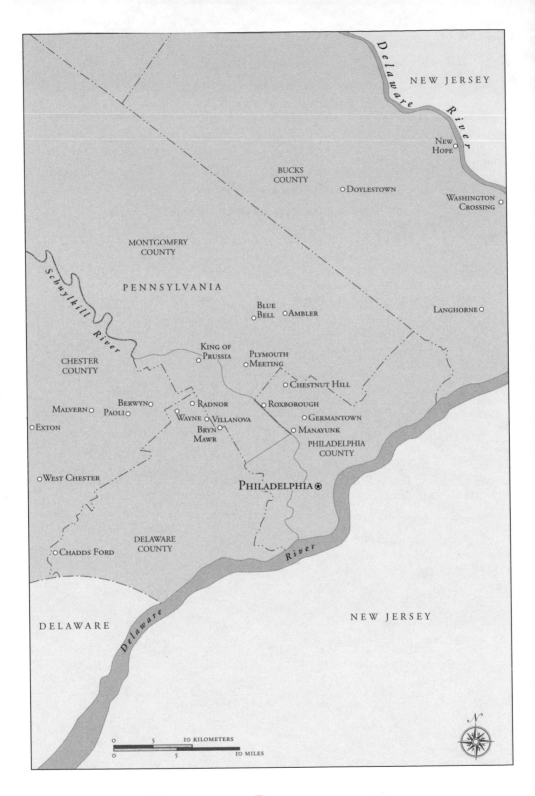

GREATER PHILADELPHIA

CONTENTS

CONTENTS

PREFACE

One of the great joys in my life was writing a book called *It Happened in Pennsylvania.* I am a history junkie and I am in love with my home state. Pennsylvania certainly has a rich and varied history. When my publisher approached me to author this book, I jumped at the opportunity. Some of the wealth of material that could not be included in the first book due to space constraints could now grace the pages of this volume.

It Happened in Philadelphia was just as much fun to write. It was exciting and fascinating to visit many of the locales described on these pages. A drive down the Schuylkill Expressway past the boathouses and into historic downtown Philadelphia has become a little dangerous for me—I can't keep from turning my head side to side to admire the many sites that these pages have brought alive for me.

My hope for this book is that I might convey some of that pleasure to the reader through my words. Perhaps I can inspire further reading on some of these intriguing stories and hopefully many visitors and locals will be motivated to visit some or all of these historic sites that all too often get taken for granted.

I also want to acknowledge that there are hundreds—no, thousands—of other stories in Philadelphia that could not be included here for many different reasons. Whether they were off topic, incongruent, or simply too short for this format is second to the main reason they were not included. There was simply not enough space.

My endeavor was to encompass as many different subjects as possible while finding some obscure tidbits that might delight and amuse the wide variety of potential readers. If I managed to accomplish any of these goals, I will consider this work to be an unconditional success. Happy reading!

ACKNOWLEDGMENTS

First and foremost, megathanks to my editors, Megan Hiller and Kaleena Cote. It is a pleasure to work with professionals. Their editing and direction were concise, practical, and enlightening.

Even a small book like this would not get completed without the help, advice, and support of many, many people. I must point out the very important contributions of my sister, Elizabeth Bruce Henning. Betsy (to all who know her) is a wonderful writer and was a real hands-on contributor to this work. Three of the chapters included here are Betsy's handiwork. I could not be more pleased or grateful for her involvement.

The ordeal of writing a book has to be shared by the author's immediate family. As always, my wife, Anne, and our children, Nick and Chloe, deserve more than just thanks; they deserve medals for putting up with me and my crazy habits. They are also invaluable critics of the work. I thank them and love them for all their input.

I would also like to show my appreciation to the members of my extended family that reside in the Philadelphia area, including my sister Joan Narkum; her husband, Dave; and the many cousins, uncles, aunts, nieces, and nephews who answered so many questions.

A very special thank you to the entire staff of the Hazleton Public Library, with special kudos to James Reimiller, Mrs. Dougherty, Mr. Neopolitan, Denise Lucadamo, and Ruth Ann Generose. More thanks and praise to the entire staff of the main branch of the Philadelphia Library, especially to the crew that helped with the microfiche machines and to Woodrow Williamson and Peggy McCullough for their help in finding some of the more obscure newspaper stories that I needed so desperately.

Michelle Henley and Brandon Zimmerman from the Mutter Museum in the College of Physicians were courteous and very helpful with my questions about Chang and Eng, the Siamese Twins. Brandon provided inside knowledge and beneficial trivia.

Thanks to "fun Mummer" Iris Cohen of the Mummer's Museum for helping with the history of the Mummers and their parade.

Big thanks to my aunt Ro Kubasik who shared her insights into the wild days of *American Bandstand*. First-hand knowledge is the most intriguing of all research. A special shout out to Michael Baldwin, aka "The Legendary Wid." One of Philadelphia's true "characters," a good friend, and a very funny man!

Finally, I would like to thank the people of Philadelphia. Everywhere I went in the city I found partners who were eager to share stories and information about the City of Brotherly Love. I truly have learned why Philadelphia gained that moniker.

GO FLY A KITE

- 1752 -

BENJAMIN FRANKLIN WAS A TRUE RENAISSANCE MAN. During his early years he was a printer, businessman, and writer. When he semi-retired from his business ventures, he turned his attention to the sciences, soon becoming a world-renowned scientist. In his later years he morphed into a statesman, playing a key role in the creation of a new nation.

Franklin spent much of his time experimenting and inventing. Among his many inventions were the Franklin stove, bifocal eyeglasses, and the glass harmonica. His study of electricity started after seeing a demonstration by a Scottish scientist in the home of a friend in Boston. The year was 1743 and the scientist was Dr. Archibald Spencer. Dr. Spencer's presentation involved creating static electricity and drawing sparks from one object to another. Franklin was enthralled.

Back home in Philadelphia, Franklin started all manner of experiments with electricity. His most important discovery at this time was that electricity had fluid properties that allowed it to flow from a positively charged component to a negatively charged component. One other important find was that electricity seemed to jump faster to a pointed object than to a blunt one. During the 1740s Franklin experimented and in fact "played" with electricity. He used his experiments to further his own knowledge and to entertain his friends. He found himself in a quandary. While he had made many great discoveries, he had yet to find any practical use for this information. After finding himself on the receiving end of a number of debilitating shocks, he proclaimed that the only use of electricity was that "it may help make a vain man humble."

In the fall of 1749 Benjamin did find one somewhat practical use for electricity: For a party he threw down by the Schuylkill River, the main course was a turkey that was executed and cooked by means of electricity.

In November 1749, Franklin noted in his science journals the similarities between lightning and his homemade sparks of electricity. Their common traits included giving off light, the color of the light, the zigzagging trajectory, swift motion, being conducted by metals, crack or noise in exploding, destroying animals, and a sulfurous smell. The twelve properties he identified would lead Franklin down the road to worldwide fame.

Up to this point in time, it had been conjectured that lightning was either a punishment from a displeased god or the work of the devil. These devastating strikes destroyed buildings, killed livestock, and created blazing fires. A common belief was that tolling the bells in the local church would help ward off the often-fatal bolts of fire. By the 1740s, however, most people had come to the conclusion that tolling the bells in church was not a proper solution to their problems. In fact churches, with their tall, pointed steeples, seemed to draw the lightning's wrath more than any other buildings.

Benjamin Franklin astutely put these facts together with what he learned from his experiments. His notes in 1749 show that he believed the water in clouds could become charged both positively and negatively with electricity. This electric charge somehow needed to be released and it naturally would be attracted to tall, pointy objects on earth such as church steeples, tall trees, and the masts of ships. His hypothesis was that a tall metal rod would attract a lightning strike that could harness the electricity and safely guide it away from buildings.

Franklin wanted to share his findings with the European scientific community. In early 1750, he sent two separate letters to Peter Collinson, a friend and agent with Franklins Library Company in London. Franklin's letters included detailed descriptions on his concept of creating a large metal tower that was specifically designed to attract lightning during a thunderstorm. He suggested that a man stand at the base of this tower in a wooden box holding a wire by means of a wax insulator for safety. Apparently Franklin believed that a man needed to be located at ground zero to fully test this theory. Back then no one realized just how dangerous this maneuver could be.

These letters were widely published and presented to the Royal Society in London, making Franklin a hero in England's scientific circles. The information was also translated into French and brought to the attention of King Louis XV early in 1752. The monarch of France showed an immediate and intense interest in the subject, and commanded his court scientists to create an experiment to prove Franklin's theories.

A king's commands do not go unheeded. A structure was erected just north of Paris and on May 10, 1752, Franklin's conjectures became facts by the crack of a lightning bolt. Electricity was passed from the clouds to a metal pole. Back in Philadelphia, Franklin was completely oblivious to his newfound fame. Word of the successful experiment spread rapidly through Europe, but news traveled pretty slowly over the Atlantic Ocean.

While Franklin was being heralded throughout the European continent, he was busy making plans to prove his theory on his own. Allegedly he was waiting for the tower of the new Christ Church located on Second Street just above Market to be erected. He planned to use the steeple as his collection point. Supposedly the delay in construction of the building led Franklin to the idea of using a childhood toy, a kite, to attract lightning instead.

Franklin made careful notes about his plan to prove that lightning was in fact electricity, and noted scientist and friend Joseph Priestly later expounded on these notes to include more scientific explanations. Franklin set up shop in a field with a small shed that was a convenient walk from town when a thunderstorm approached. On a day that showed tumultuous skies with the potential for thunder and lightning, the forty-six-year-old Franklin headed out of town with his twenty-one-year-old son William.

Speculation suggests that Franklin wanted this experiment kept quiet and that was why he used his son as his assistant. The kite he used was different from the normal toy in several ways. A metal wire was attached to the kite frame to act as a lightning rod, and the kite was constructed of silk, which Franklin thought would hold up better than paper in the wet weather. A simple key was attached to the bottom of the kite string, which was made of hemp. A separate wire would be held near the key to see if sparks would jump from one to the other.

The kite was flown in the clouds for some time with no excitement at all. No bolts of lightning struck the kite. Unknown to Ben and William, this probably proved to be fortuitous. A direct lightning strike would have been extremely dangerous and possibly fatal.

What the elder Franklin did notice was a stiffening of the threads of loose hemp kite string. By placing his knuckle near the key, Ben was able to draw sparks.

He had a Leyden jar—a device designed to store electricity—along for just this type of success. He had made the jar after seeing other scientists use one to store static electricity. The jar was made of glass with a metal foil wrapped around the outside. Inside the jar was water, lead, or some other metal that could hold an electric charge. The glass acted as an insulator between the metal foil outside and the conductor inside. A simple wire could feed electricity into the jar. Ben Franklin collected electricity from lightning in his Leyden jar.

Back home he conducted experiments that showed the collected storm electricity had the same properties as his own manufactured electricity. Ben Franklin had taken the experiment full circle, proving his own theory completely. All of this occurred approximately a month after the successful French experiment, but before Franklin heard about it.

Although the experiment took place in June 1752, Franklin's findings were not published until that fall. This delay has led some historians to doubt Franklin's claim. Why didn't he publish sooner? Why was the experiment conducted in secret? Is it possible that he fabricated the kite story?

The facts seem to contradict any possibility that this was a hoax. First, no records anywhere have shown that Franklin ever contrived or embellished any of his scientific facts. In addition, Ben's partner that day was his son William. Many years after the kite experiment, William and his father had a horrible fight that put them on different sides during the American Revolution. Their disagreement was filled with such animosity that it is hard to believe that the young man wouldn't take the opportunity to discredit his father if he knew the famous kite experiment to be a false claim.

Franklin regularly took his time submitting his scientific reports. It seems he wanted to make sure of his facts and to compose a complete report. He might have conducted his experiment in secrecy for fear of looking foolish. The Franklin theory of electricity had many detractors. It is unlikely that the esteemed Mr. Franklin would want to provide more grist for their mills.

Noted historian I. Bernard Cohen researched this subject thoroughly and debunked the whole issue of a Franklin hoax in his 1990 book titled *Benjamin Franklin's Science*. He noted that Franklin did not claim his experiment took place before the French one. Indeed, Franklin freely acknowledged that the French proved his theory before he did. If in fact he was trying to take credit, wouldn't he have moved the event to a date prior to the French experiment? Cohen's last tidbit may be the most telling piece of information. The very first lightning rods in the world were erected in Philadelphia by late June or early July of 1752. The news of the success in France would have just been reaching America. It seems obvious that Franklin's experiments led to the use of these lightning rods.

All of these details lead to a clear story: Flying a kite with his son in a field near the Philadelphia city limits during the month of June 1752 proved Benjamin Franklin's theory that lightning was electricity.

One final note: Benjamin Franklin received honorary degrees from both Harvard and Yale in 1753 for his body of work with electricity. That same year, London's Royal Society bestowed an even more impressive honor—the gold Copley Medal. This award was as prestigious as winning a Nobel Prize is today.

THE TRANSIT OF VENUS

- 1769 -

IT WAS A CLEAR, SUNNY DAY IN Philadelphia on June 3, 1769. And that more than anything else made it a spectacular day for David Rittenhouse and the American Philosophical Society. This society, and Rittenhouse in particular, was charged with the auspicious job of observing and learning from that day's exciting astronomical event, one that would not occur again until 1874, 105 years in the future. Astronomers around the world were waiting in giddy anticipation for the transit of Venus, when Venus's orbit would place that planet directly between the Sun and Earth.

Astronomy was truly in its infancy in 1769. While humans had studied the stars since the beginning of time, very little precise scientific knowledge was available about even our own solar system. Exact distances between planets and the Sun were unknown, and it was hoped that the transit of Venus would somehow shed more light on that subject.

Venus stirred up so much excitement among astronomers because it is the third brightest natural object visible from Earth's surface;

only the Sun and Moon are brighter. The proximity of this particular event would naturally be easier to see and document than any occurence involving more distant heavenly bodies. Venus has long been called either the "morning star" or the "evening star" because of its prominence in the sky.

The official and professional astronomers of the royal courts of Europe determined that the American Atlantic seaboard would be the ideal position on the planet to observe the transit. Two of the most respected of these astronomers were Englishmen Mason and Dixon. These men had already gained a great deal of fame for their work surveying the boundary between Pennsylvania and Maryland. Mason and Dixon set off by ship to make their own observations of the transit from the southern hemisphere. Unfortunately the team never reached their planned destination—a French frigate attacked their ship, ultimately causing them to miss the big event.

The American Philosophical Society was at that time one of the most prestigious scientific organizations in the world. The founder of the society, the ubiquitous Benjamin Franklin, headed the group. It was through his efforts that the organization obtained the financial backing to be involved in this scientific phenomenon. A sum of one hundred pounds was pried from the government coffers to build a small observatory right on the State House lawn in downtown Philadelphia. The funds also allowed for the purchase of a reflecting telescope and a micrometer. These instruments were to be procured from England by Franklin.

David Rittenhouse was already an important man in Philadelphia. He was descended from William Rittenhouse, who built the first paper mill in America in the 1600s. In addition to being a member of the American Philosophical Society, David was also a skilled maker of fine precision mechanical instruments including clocks.

Rittenhouse set up a second observatory in the town of Norriton just north and east of Philadelphia. For this very special day Rittenhouse designed and built his own transit telescope with spider-web crosshairs, a quadrant, and a pendulum clock. These tools allowed Mr. Rittenhouse to make fairly accurate measurements of the distance between Earth and Venus. His hope was that this information would allow him to extrapolate the distance between Earth and the Sun.

When the big day finally arrived, the Philadelphia astronomers found themselves very well prepared. It has been stated that David Rittenhouse fell into a near faint with excitement. The record shows that he rallied to the occasion and as Venus moved in front of the Sun, he began taking measurements between the centers of the two bodies at timed intervals.

At the exact moment that Venus centered in front of the Sun, Rittenhouse noticed a glowing circle that evenly surrounded the planet. Only one conclusion could be drawn from this observation: Venus had an atmosphere, just like Earth. This was very heady stuff, and one of the most important discoveries in astronomical history. It had been suggested in the past that Venus might have an atmosphere, but this observation virtually proved that hypothesis. It opened a world of new questions: Could the planet Venus support life? Was it possible that we were not alone in the universe? The scientific community would have a lot to chew on for the next one hundred years.

Rittenhouse went on to publish all of his findings. He listed his conclusions about the atmosphere of Venus and his calculations of distances both to Venus and the Sun. Over the course of time Rittenhouse's computations proved to be surprisingly accurate. His work placed him in the company of the leading astronomers of his day.

An unnamed authority in England was quoted as saying, "The first approximately accurate results in the measurements of the spheres were given to the world, not by schooled and salaried astronomers who watched from the magnificent royal observatories of Europe, but by unpaid amateurs and devotees to science in the youthful province of Pennsylvania."

It was this type of recognition that helped put America on a worldwide stage in the field of science. Rittenhouse went on to make observations of the transit of Mercury and is often credited with the invention of the practical planetarium which most closely resembles the planetariums of today. When Benjamin Franklin passed away in 1791, David Rittenhouse succeeded that giant of mankind as the president of the prestigious American Philosophical Society. He held that position until his own demise and was replaced by none other than Thomas Jefferson.

A HOUSEWIFE SPY COMPLETES
HER MISSION

- 1777 -

ON JULY 20, 1777, BRITISH GENERAL SIR WILLIAM HOWE LED fourteen thousand troops by boat from New York Harbor to a landing below Philadelphia in a quest to capture that city. After successful campaigns against Washington and his ragtag army in Brandywine to the south and Germantown to the north, Howe settled in to occupy the colonial capital.

Philadelphia in 1777 was a thriving city. In fact it was not only one of the preeminent cities in America, it was one of the principal "English" cities in the world. Howe immediately commandeered homes in the affluent eastern part of the city near the Delaware River to set up his headquarters. In late September, he personally took over the home of American General Cadwalader, who was a close friend of Washington's. This home was just across the street from the home of William and Lydia Darragh on Second Street.

These homes were fairly representative of the well-to-do of the times. They were constructed with four rooms and a kitchen out back as well as an attic. William and Lydia had the additional luxury of a large extra room located in the rear of their home. This room would become the downfall of Howe.

Shortly after settling into his new headquarters, Howe sent men around the neighborhood to scout more homes to quarter his officers. When soldiers showed up at her door, Lydia—a mousy, fiftyish housewife—was in despair. The British officers gave the family only one hour to pack up and vacate. Lydia's family was composed of herself, her husband, and four children living at home. The eldest, Ann, was twenty, but the younger children were just fourteen, eleven, and nine. Lydia could not imagine dragging her children out into the freezing night with nowhere to go.

Gathering her courage, she approached the officer at her door and offered him a hot cup of tea. This act of kindness was well received and allowed Lydia to begin a conversation with the soldier. They discovered they were both born in Ireland and Lydia used this connection to ingratiate herself even further. She begged for his mercy and ultimately received a stay that would allow her family to remain. The younger children were packed off to relatives in the country. A bargain was struck that would allow the British to use the large room to the rear of the house as their council hall.

Howe had no reason to suspect the Darraghs. William and Lydia were Quakers in good standing with their sect. The Quakers were and are opposed to war in all forms and were self-proclaimed neutrals in the war for independence. In fact many Quakers were incorrectly believed to be Tories since they refused to become involved in the war effort. Howe assumed that these particular Quakers were of this mold.

Perhaps Howe would have thought twice if he had been aware that William and Lydia had another, older son, Charles, who was not living at home. This young man was in fact a member of General

George Washington's army. The love for her son and her belief in American independence moved Lydia into the opposition camp despite her religious beliefs.

Charles Darragh, along with General Washington and the rest of the beleaguered American army, was camped north of the city in Whitemarsh. Washington had been creating his spy network since the beginning of the hostilities. Most sympathizers were aware of this network and Lydia became an integral part. Not only were there bits and pieces of information to pick up around the neighborhood, but now she had gabbing soldiers right in her own parlor. Lydia would take notes, and William would transcribe them into a shorthand code. These notes would then get sewn into buttons and placed on the coat of their fourteen-year-old son, John. John would be sent on some imaginary errand and once out of town would get the messages to his brother Charles or some other connection in the underground network.

These activities continued until one night in December, when the information Lydia gathered would bring her directly into the line of fire. The evening of December 2 started as many did during that period in the Darragh household. Soldiers came into the house and ordered everyone to bed—the council was meeting. After an appropriate period of time, Lydia crept from her bed and slowly opened her creaking bedroom door. She took refuge in a closet that shared a wall with the council chamber. Pressing her ear to the wall, she was able to discern that the British were planning a sneak attack on Whitemarsh.

The British plan was to travel at night on the fourth and attack Washington unawares. The prevailing belief was that they could wipe out the entire army with a surprise attack and end this nuisance uprising in one fell swoop.

Lydia snuck back to bed with her mind reeling. Not only would this be a fatal blow to freedom, but her son Charles would certainly be in grave danger. A short while later, a soldier knocked—perhaps someone had heard the creaking door—and a disheveled Lydia feigned sleepiness as she explained that she and her husband had been fast asleep.

All day on the third, Lydia struggled with this new information. She did not share the knowledge with her husband, and she didn't feel right about sending a fourteen-year-old boy with such explosive information through the enemy lines. What could she do?

By nightfall she had her plan. She told her husband that she needed flour from the mill in Germantown and planned a day trip: She would walk to Germantown, get her flour, and then visit with relatives since she would be nearby. No one knew of her true intentions. She would not need an incriminating note as she carried the firsthand information in her head.

Early on the morning of the fourth, Lydia Darragh set out into the cold dawn on her spy mission. She had her empty flour sack, her special pass issued by General Howe, and her plain Quaker clothing.

Over an hour of travel by foot would bring her to the first sentinel posted for security. There were many of these posts and Lydia passed through each with trepidation, as suspicions were high among the British. Many residents of Philadelphia had to make this trek to the mills, so it was widely used by Washington's spies. Unfortunately no one knew Lydia was coming so there was no one to meet her.

By the time she reached the Frankford mill in Germantown, Lydia had walked five miles in the freezing December cold. The good news was that she was safely outside the British zone of influence. The bad news was that she had many miles yet to traverse to deliver her message and many more miles to return. Her feet were cold and she was tired. But the thought of her son, and indeed independence itself, drove her on.

Lydia aimed to the west on a path toward the intersection of Old York and Germantown Roads. Here she knew she would find a known hangout for American spies known as the Rising Sun Tavern. Fortune was with Lydia on that road. She happened upon a traveler on horseback, who was not only a sympathizer, but also an acquaintance. American Colonel Craig got down from his horse and walked with Lydia as she unloaded her secret burden onto his shoulders.

The grateful colonel took Lydia to a local farmhouse and ordered the family to feed her and allow her to rest. Craig rode off to inform Washington of the impending attack.

After a short respite, Lydia began her arduous journey home. Seven miles of terrain still had to be crossed, with a twenty-five-pound sack of flour to weigh her down. She knew that she had completed her portion of this task, but there was no way to know if it would be a success. Anxiety would be her close companion for the next few days. While the attack was scheduled for that very night, there was no way for Lydia to ask about the outcome without revealing her knowledge of the British Army's plans. The days crawled by with no new information.

Colonel Craig did in fact get the vital information to General Washington. This information corroborated and crystallized other intelligence already gathered by Washington's network, and he immediately mobilized his men and prepared for the oncoming attack.

Howe and his armies were robbed of the element of surprise, and after a few small skirmishes the British fighting force had no choice but to give up and go back to the safe environs of Philadelphia with their tails between their legs. This crucial turning point in the war allowed Washington to regroup and go on to claim victory for the United States.

Word eventually got back to Lydia Darragh that her efforts helped win the day. As time passed, the British would leave and her life would return to normal, but for that short period of time the little Quaker housewife from Second Street was a super spy.

MESCHIANZA

- 1778 -

WHILE THE WINTER OF 1777–1778 WAS A MISERABLE, dreary experience for George Washington and his troops camped at Valley Forge, it was a time of party and comfort for General Howe and his British Army in Philadelphia. Howe and his men were under no real threat from the Revolutionary forces. They had secured the Delaware River in the fall and thus had safe passage for supplies. The Brits took this break in the fighting to play in our new nation's capital. They set cricket matches, attended the theater, arranged dances, gambled, and in general just had a plain old good time.

Benjamin Franklin commented on the scene publicly. He claimed that "Howe did not take Philadelphia—Philadelphia took Howe."

Word of Howe's indiscretions and lack of military decorum crossed the Atlantic; Howe's superiors were not amused and passed along a rebuke. General Howe regarded the rebuke as unfair and promptly resigned his commission. Arrangements were made for his replacement in the person of Sir Henry Clinton.

Howe and his chief officers made the decision to go out with a bang. They were not just going to throw a party . . . they were going to have a Meschianza! Of course that begs the question, what exactly is a Meschianza? It seems to be a made-up word, possibly having roots in the Italian word *mescolanza,* meaning "to mix." In this case the word Meschianza meant a gala event that included multiple facets.

The concept of the daylong party may have been the brainchild of Major John Andre, who was the primary coordinator and chief architect of the event. This bash had to be organized in a big hurry—there were only about thirty days for preparation. And a lot of preparation was needed, since the blueprint for the occasion included a regatta, dances, marching bands, a jousting tournament, poetry readings, fireworks, and a feast.

More than twenty of the wealthiest officers under Howe's command chipped in £140 each in a massive show of affection for their leader. This was a lot of money, and Major Andre carefully spent it all. He designed the costumes that would be worn by the ladies and knights of the joust. He spelled out the construction needed for the great lawn at the mansion of Joseph Wharton. He also drew up designs for the flowery floats and craft that would make up the regatta. Andre even lent his hand to the motif of the individual handmade invitations.

The fun started in uptown Philadelphia with an overcast morning. The May sun fought its way through the cloud cover and by noon the partygoers had a perfect day. Guests boarded a variety of vessels at Knight's Wharf. All of the flatboats and party craft were decorated from stern to bow, and at least one barge carried a marine band that played music as the regatta proceeded down the Delaware River. The shore was packed with town folk observing and admiring the outlandish spectacle.

The short jaunt on the river ended at Wharton's property just south of the city, where the guests disembarked and strolled through the grounds. There was bleacher seating erected for the tournament. As the crowd of approximately four hundred settled in, they inspected the arches that were built for the bout.

In a timely fashion the tournament with all its pomp and circumstance began. The young ladies whose favor the knights were battling for occupied the front seats for the spectacle. The knights were actually British Army officers and the ladies were mostly daughters of prominent Philadelphians who were sympathetic to the Tory cause. There were two "teams" in the competition. The seven white knights were dressed in white and red silks and mounted on gray steeds. They were called the "Knights of the Blended Rose" and their chief was Lord Cathcart. The "Knights of the Burning Mountain" or the black knights were handsomely decked out in silks of black and orange with black horses. The chief of the black knights was Captain Watson. The ladies corresponding to each set of knights were garbed in color-coordinated silks of their own. They were also decorated with "favors" for their heroes.

A trumpet heralded the arrival of the knights to the tilting field. One chief threw down the gauntlet, which was promptly retrieved by his opponent, and the games were under way. Each knight made a number of passes against his counterpart. Jousting poles were used for show. Pistols were shot into the air and mock sword fights entertained the crowd. Finally the two chiefs squared off in a dramatic semi-serious battle. Major Gwynne, who played the part of "Marshall of the Field," cut this scuffle short. The Marshall proclaimed that the ladies were sufficiently impressed so that the fighting could cease.

More entertainments ensued including music, dancing, and poetry. The party pushed on past dark and participants moved indoors. At 10 p.m. the windows were opened to a vista of fireworks.

Captain Montresor, the chief engineer, was charged with this portion of the evening; it was reported that he achieved great success. The fireworks were also enjoyed from afar by the town folk who were not lucky enough to be invited to the fete.

As midnight approached, the guests prepared for the feast. It was reported to be the most sumptuous meal ever served in Philadelphia. More music, dancing, and revelry followed dinner, and the party lasted through dawn.

Most reviews of the evening by participants were very positive. It was one heck of a party. The British Press was less impressed. Loyalist Joseph Galloway wrote, "We have seen the same General, with a vanity and presumption unparalleled in history, after this indolence, after all these wretched blunders, accept from a few of his officers a triumph more magnificent than would have become the conqueror of America, without the consent of his sovereign or approbation of his country, and that at a time when the news of war with France had just arrived, and in the very city, the capital of North America, the late seat of Congress, which in a few days was to be delivered up to that Congress."

The general view was that Sir William Howe and his officers had accomplished nothing to celebrate, much less celebrate in such high style. Time has been generous to the perpetrators of this event. While most historians still consider the extravaganza to be over the top for a displaced general, that majority also agrees that the Meschianza has lasted through history as a wonderful sample of Philadelphia folklore.

THE DOANS ARE DONE

- 1787 -

THE FIRST GREAT CRIMINALS OF THE NEWLY formed United States of America were the members of the Doan Gang, a colorful group of brothers and others whose tales weave through the Revolutionary War and beyond. Not only were they common criminals, they were Tory sympathizers and in certain circles somewhat heroic.

From all accounts the Doan boys were rough customers even in their youth. They were the bullies of the countryside just north of Philadelphia. One reason they were able to bully others was the simple truth that they were the strongest and most athletic boys for miles around—once the boys became infamous, friends and acquaintances from their formative years attested to this fact. These associates described gatherings of boys from around the area to compete in various athletic endeavors. The Doan brothers won all contests in running, jumping, wrestling, and pretty much everything else. On top of that, they were good-looking and popular.

The oldest Doan boy was Moses. He was also the biggest and the toughest. The only boy from the neighborhood who posed a challenge to Moses was William Hart, who was tenacious in their wrestling bouts but never managed to best the larger Moses. Hart was to become a nemesis for the Doan brothers in later years.

Moses had four brothers: Aaron, Levi, Mahlon, and Joseph. They all shared the same physical appearance and abilities, and a cousin, Abraham Doan, fit this same mold. Although others would periodically join the group, these boys would form the heart of the infamous Doan Gang.

Researchers have uncovered the series of incidents that seems to have led the boys down the wrong path. One key piece of information has to do with the boys' rural upbringing. In those unsteady days before the Revolution, members of the farming communities did not share their city cousins' displeasure with the King of England. The taxes that were being handed down to the colonies had a much greater effect on city dwellers and merchants than on the self-contained agricultural population. Farmers' taxes came from local government, not the king, so the farmers tended to side with the crown in that debate.

It was in this atmosphere that young Moses Doan had a disagreement with his father. The fight escalated to the point that Moses left home, vowing not to return, in the fall of 1770. After leaving home Moses found himself in an Indian skirmish that allowed him to play hero, saving a family of settlers. Moses took an extreme liking to the daughter of that family, but his romantic advances were rebuffed. This combination of events and circumstances pushed Moses to join a local band of Wolf Indians.

Most of the remaining Indians in the area were pretty agitated with the white settlers during those times. They felt that their lands had been encroached upon and it was common to hear of Indian raids against the settlers. Although Moses probably did not participate in any of these raids, he did grow his hair long and live with these raiders.

Moses spent more than a year with the Wolf Indians. How much effect this time with these renegades had on Moses is pure conjecture. However, what is known for a fact is that Moses recruited his brothers shortly after his time with the Indians and started his own group of raiders.

The gang of Doan brothers held up tax collectors and stole horses from rebel patriots. They found willing buyers for the horses in neighboring Philadelphia, where the loyalists to the Crown saw nothing wrong in the gang's methods. As tensions increased between loyalist Tories and American Patriots, Moses and his band sided more and more with the Tories. By the time war broke out, Moses had become an invaluable spy for the Armies of England.

Moses Doan, his brothers, cousin, and followers had become extremely well known all over Southeastern Pennsylvania, New Jersey, and Delaware for their daring raids. They became expert at disguises and stealth. Moses took to traveling far from home, especially as it pertained to his spying activities. He hooked up with General Howe of the British Army and there is some proof that his spying was one of the main factors in General Washington's defeat on Long Island.

This brand of infamy led to a more national notoriety for Moses and all the Doans: They became hunted men with bounties on their heads. However, there were also stories of Moses that led some people to believe he was a heroic figure, and he gained a reputation as a modern Robin Hood. While this reputation was not wholly earned, there are instances that support it.

A prime example is the story of a young woman whose husband was camped with Washington at Valley Forge. She had no food for her starving children, yet the English authorities refused to give her a pass to travel to the mills for flour and other important staples. Desperate, she took off on foot and managed to purchase some necessary provisions. On her way home, exhausted from her trip, she crossed paths with Moses Doan. Upon hearing the poor woman's story, Moses not only gave her his purse, he also warned her of the next sentry's location. He then slipped off into the night. As the woman progressed on her journey, a British sentry accosted her. This encounter was not so pleasant. After hearing her story and verifying that she had no pass, the soldier took her sack of flour forcefully. At that moment an elderly man trundled out of the woods. The woman claims to have recognized her earlier benefactor immediately. The man asked the sentry to return the flour and even offered to pay for it. The soldier's refusal was the biggest mistake of his life. The elderly man showed a quickness that betrayed his appearance. Moses Doan grabbed the guard, returned the property of the woman, and shot the man in cold blood. The woman was able to return home during the confusion as the British gathered up to chase Moses. In the process of his escape, Doan killed another guard and later shot a British officer. And just like all his other previous raids and crimes, he got away.

This ability to vanish into the night and his many exploits as a spy landed Moses Doan a nickname with the British: Eagle Spy. Eagle Spy had one more great adventure that could easily have changed the outcome of the Revolutionary War. Moses was spying as always in December 1776. He noticed troop movements that led him to believe that Washington might be planning an attack against the British forces in Trenton. While patrolling the area known as McKonkey's Ferry, now called Washington Crossing, he saw a gathering of ferry boats. Moses correctly surmised on that Christmas Eve day that Washington was planning a surprise attack. Doan rode north and crossed the Delaware River in a violent snowstorm. He then turned south and rode all the way to Trenton well ahead of the invading army. Upon his arrival he asked to speak with the commander, a Colonel Rahl.

The Colonel refused to be disturbed, as he was playing a card game. This was his first monumental mistake. Then Doan wrote a note to be given to the Colonel. The note said, "Washington is coming on you down the river, he will be here afore long. Doan." Apparently Rahl then made his second monumental mistake: He put the unread note in his vest pocket, where it was found the next day after the battle was over. The single most important piece of espionage work in the entire war went unused.

Doan and his gang were now superstars or super-enemies, depending on where your loyalties lie. They were all well-known and recognizable figures. How they eluded capture is incomprehensible. There were large sums of money on their heads and they had a number of military people searching everywhere for them.

One of those who doggedly kept after them was none other than Colonel William Hart—the same William Hart who had wrestled the Doan boys back in their youth. By this time Moses and his cousin Abraham were the leaders of the gang. They found themselves ranging farther and farther from their home territory to accomplish their nefarious deeds. They were literally being hounded by the authorities.

As the midpoint of the 1780s passed, the Doans were running out of options and friends. The war was over, so there was no support from the loyalists. The crimes of the gang had become too violent for most people. Joseph Doan was shot and captured during the robbery of a tavern and was subsequently hanged in Philadelphia. The rest of the outlaws knew what fate awaited them.

Moses, his brother Levi, and cousin Abraham were hiding out at the Halsey farm near Fleecydale Road just north of Philadelphia. The family sent their eleven-year-old son to the mill on the Delaware River to obtain flour to feed the bandits. The boy may have bragged or just been careless in mentioning that the Doans were at his house. This information made its way to the Gardenville Tavern, where one of the patrons put down his beer when he heard the news. It was Colonel William Hart.

Hart gathered seven men for reinforcements and rushed to the Halsey Farm. He erupted into the room and immediately set to wrestling with Moses Doan. Maybe Moses was tired from all the running and hiding. Maybe Hart had become a better wrestler. In any event, Moses Doan soon surrendered. As Moses was giving up, a newcomer to the fracas, Captain Robert Gibson of Fisherville, took aim and shot the bandit in the chest. Moses Doan was killed instantly.

Levi and Abraham Doan escaped in the confusion but not without imparting more violence. In the escape a Major Kennedy was wounded and later died of those wounds. Moses's body was snatched up by a local man and ridden to the home of his parents, where he was dumped unceremoniously in their yard. His burial spot is unknown to this day.

It is believed that Mahlon Doan somehow made his escape to England. Abraham and Levi Doan did not fare as well. They were arrested on May 15, 1787, just west of Philadelphia in Chester County. The pair were jailed in Philadelphia and sentenced to be hanged for their crimes. Their time in prison was not uneventful; they made numerous escape attempts. Abraham's sister, Mary Doan, attempted to pass a saw and a file to the outlaws by cleverly baking the items into a loaf of bread. That plot was unsuccessful, but amazingly she returned to the jail the very same day disguised as an elderly Quaker woman. This time she succeeded in passing a file to her brother. The men were hanged on September 24, 1787, before they were able to make full use of the file.

Mary got custody of the remains of her brother and cousin, but the Quakers refused her request to bury the men in their cemetery, so they were laid to rest just outside the cemetery walls. That marked the end of the reign of terror and espionage of the Doan Gang.

FIRST IN LIBERTY; FIRST IN ROBBERY

- 1798 -

Philadelphia is famous for its many "firsts." From the first public library to the first computer, the city can boast numerous inventions and accomplishments. Philadelphia can also lay claim to the first bank robbery in the United States.

Sometime during the night of Saturday, August 31, 1798, two men entered Carpenters' Hall at 320 Chestnut Street in downtown Philadelphia. In addition to being the oldest trade guild in America, Carpenters' Hall was at that time the landlord for the Bank of Pennsylvania. The bank was physically located in the hall. These two men proceeded to cart off a record haul of $162,821.61—the equivalent of approximately $1.8 million today! The thieves left no clues other than the fact that nothing was broken: The locks were not jimmied and there were no signs of forced entry. This led the police to believe that it was an inside job.

This burglary had the potential to be the perfect crime. It didn't turn out that way, though, for the same reason most crimes are not successful: At least one of the criminals was an idiot. But there is much more to this story than just a dumb crook.

Philadelphia was under siege during the summer of 1798. Yellow fever had once again invaded the city and took close to 1,300 lives that year. One of the victims of the fever was also one of the bank robbers, Thomas Cunningham, the "inside man" on the heist. Cunningham had a job at Carpenters' Hall and also slept there on occasion. He may very well have already been infected with yellow fever at the time of the crime. Cunningham died from the disease in early September. With the "inside man" out of the picture, his partner would get away with this crime scot-free . . . if he just lay low.

The second player in this drama was not smart enough to recognize his own fortune. Isaac Davis was also a member of the Carpenters' Company. It is believed that he was from somewhere other than Philadelphia, but there is no record of where that might be. Shortly after the bank job he started making large deposits of cash in various banks in and around Philadelphia. One of those institutions of finance was astoundingly the very bank he robbed, the Bank of Pennsylvania.

While Davis was running around proving his lack of common sense, another drama was unfolding. The police charged with the investigation, immediately suspecting that this was an "inside" job, turned their attentions to local blacksmith Patrick Lyon, a tall, muscular, and well respected craftsman. When the Bank of Pennsylvania moved its operation into Carpenters' Hall that summer, they hired Lyon to adapt their old iron bank-vault doors to fit their new home. Of course this job included the forging of the new key to the vault doors. He was in a hurry to complete this job because he wanted to get out of town, away from the dreaded plague, as many other residents were doing. Lyon finished his job, packed up his apprentice, and fled south to the Delaware shore.

Lyon made the key and Lyon left town. These two undisputed facts led Constable John Haines and a number of bank officials to name Lyon as their number one suspect. A cry went up and soon the surrounding countrysides of Pennsylvania, New Jersey, and Delaware were being searched for the redheaded Patrick Lyon.

Down in Delaware, Lyon was not having a very nice retreat. His young apprentice and traveling companion had not gotten out of Philadelphia soon enough: The nineteen-year-old man had contracted yellow fever and quickly succumbed to the disease.

Lyon was monitoring the Philadelphia news to ascertain the status of the plague. He quickly learned that he was a suspect in an unbelievable bank heist back in town. Lyon wasted no time at all: He packed up and headed home to clear his name. He took a boat from Lewistown (now Lewes) to Wilmington, Delaware, and then walked the remaining twenty miles to Philadelphia. Upon his arrival in the City of Brotherly Love, he was immediately arrested and thrown in jail. Constable Haines was more interested in his two-thousand-dollar reward than searching for the truth.

By this time Isaac Davis was raising eyebrows all over town with his large cash deposits. When this piece of information made its way to the authorities, they decided it might be a good idea to pull him in for questioning. That was all it took. Isaac Davis folded like a cheap suit, immediately confessing to his involvement and giving up his dead partner, Thomas Cunningham, as well. He explained that Thomas Cunningham had access to the key and the two simply slipped in, bagged the money, and slipped right back out. Amazingly, Mr. Davis evaded all prosecution. He did not spend even one day in jail. He agreed to return the money, and the only punishment he received was being unceremoniously dumped out of the Carpenters' Company.

Meanwhile, Lyon was still in jail. Although Davis had completely exonerated Lyon, bank authorities could not be convinced of his innocence. Lyon was stuck in a cold, damp four-by-twelve-foot cell on Walnut Street in the middle of a city that was being ravaged by yellow fever. He truly feared for his life. Prosecutors asked for and got an unheard-of $150,000 bail. No blacksmith of the era would be able to raise that amount, so Lyon wasted away in prison for three long, miserable months.

No proof of Lyon's involvement in the crime was ever found and finally the courts realized they had imprisoned an innocent man. Upon his release Lyons set out to write a book about his experience. The book was eventually published with an unbelievable title: *Narrative of Patrick Lyon Who Suffered Three Months Severe Imprisonment in Philadelphia Gaol on Merely a Vague Suspicion of Being Concerned in a Robbery of the Bank of Pennsylvania With his Remarks Thereon.* The title nearly tells the whole story.

Davis had long since left Philadelphia but failed to return all the money. Two thousand dollars were never accounted for. Lyon was a bitter man and he demanded justice. He began civil proceedings against the bank. The trial was memorable for many reasons. The top lawyers in Philadelphia participated in the court case, and the tribulations of Patrick Lyon were mapped out for the jury and judge. The whole city followed the trial just as they had followed the news of the robbery. In the end the jury awarded Lyon a sum of twelve thousand dollars for his mistreatment. The Bank of Pennsylvania appealed but eventually settled out of court for nine thousand dollars.

This was a very princely sum at the end of the eighteenth century. Patrick Lyon would go back to his blacksmithing, but he was now a man of means and went on to live a comfortable life. Isaac Davis disappeared into history and was not heard from again. Carpenters' Hall still stands on Walnut Street in Philadelphia and is open to visitors. Please don't steal anything!

THE RIOTS OF 1844

- 1844 -

THE SCENE IN PHILADELPHIA DURING THE 1840S was a tumultuous one, politically speaking. The United States of America was undergoing a lot of changes. There was an immigration boom and many foreigners were settling in Philadelphia; the largest incoming group was the Irish Catholics. One of the key political issues of the day revolved around the use of the Bible in public schools. The Catholics objected to the use of the Protestant King James Bible and believed their children should be taught with the Catholic version instead.

On the other side of this conflict were the Protestant Native Americans, not to be confused with the group we currently call Native Americans or American Indians. This group was made up of people, mainly of English heritage, who could trace their roots back to the days before the American Revolution. The Nativists were concerned that these foreigners were able to obtain citizenship quite easily—as their numbers grew, their political power would surely increase, and eventually these foreigners would be able to make widespread changes. The Nativists took a very dim view of Catholics and the issue over the Bible took center stage.

These Nativists felt that their own Democratic Party was becoming too sympathetic to the Irish cause. Many left the party to join the Whigs. Others started a new party called the American Republicans. This new party had a simple three-plank platform:

1. To extend the period of naturalization
2. To elect none but natives to office
3. To reject foreign interference in all our institutions, social, religious, and political

Minor confrontations were taking place around Philadelphia during the first few months of 1844. Tempers were reaching a boiling point by May of that year.

On the third of May, the new American Republican Party had arranged a rally to be held in the Third Ward, Kensington District, the heart of the Irish immigrant population of the city. The rally, which only drew about a hundred people, was disrupted by Irish hecklers. The Republicans fled south to the community of Northern Liberties, which separated Kensington from downtown Philadelphia. The remaining Irish tore down the speaker's platform and carted the lumber to their homes for firewood.

The American Republicans decided to draw a line in the sand over this incident. They planned a second rally for Monday, May 6, on the same site. Another speaker's stand was erected in the school-yard at the intersection of Second and Master Streets. The Republicans papered the town with flyers extolling the virtues of their platform and its controversial planks. Three thousand people showed up that Monday afternoon. It is unclear how many people in the crowd were pro-Republican and how many were pro-Irish, but both sides were represented.

The speeches began around 3:30 p.m. after a ceremonial flag raising. Native American Samuel Kramer finished the speech he had begun the previous Friday. The second speaker was Peter Sken Smith, a colonel in the militia, editor of the *Dailey Sun,* a temperance lecturer, and one of the organizers of the American Republican Party. It was during Smith's lecture that the first major disruption occurred.

Irish carter John O'Neil drove his wagon through the crowd and right up to the speaker's platform. He dumped the contents of his wagon, which was either dirt or manure, about ten feet from Colonel Smith. There is no doubt as to the intended insult. While this was probably an attempt to cause a ruckus, it did not achieve that purpose. The very next speaker was Lewis Levin, who "soldiered on" with the proceedings while O'Neil drove his rig away. (Levin was Jewish, an interesting choice of speaker for this Protestant-based organization.)

During Levin's speech a rain cloud burst forth and that more than anything else was the cause for the ensuing violence. The crowd dispersed, with most running for the shelter of the Nanny Goat Market. The Republicans decided to attempt to continue in the market, but a group of Irish residents were determined to stop the rally immediately. A *Philadelphia Ledger* reporter claimed he heard an Irishman yell, "Keep the damned natives out of the market house; this ground don't belong to them, it's ours!"

Levin attempted to conclude his remarks, but Irish hecklers continued to interrupt. Shouts turned to blows. Suddenly there were bricks, clubs, and even guns appearing in what were once empty hands. The fighting was vicious. Those who attempted to stop the fighting paid a price for their good intentions, such as Patrick Fisher, who was Irish and a former constable in the Kensington community. As he stepped between two rioters, he was shot in the face.

The Republicans outnumbered the Irish in the market house and soon gained the upper hand in the fighting. But as the melee moved outdoors, that advantage disappeared. The Republicans were fighting on foreign soil. The Irish were positioned in their houses and rained musket shot and anything they could throw down upon their adversaries.

Some of the Republicans withdrew back down to Northern Liberties, where they gathered reinforcements and more firepower. They returned to the fray with a vengeance. The battle raged on with one side getting an upper hand then the other fighting back. At about five o'clock Sheriff McMichael and his deputies arrived on the scene. The hour-long clash came to an uneasy end for the day.

There were only two recorded deaths of Republicans and no recorded Irish deaths. It is believed there were over fifty serious injuries. The Natives seemed to take pride in the fact that instead of killing they had only destroyed Irish homes.

The next day brought more mayhem. The Republicans had printed handbills that called for the people to rise up and fight "the bloody hand of the Pope." The American Republicans set out to do as much damage as they could. They burned Irish houses, Saint Michael's Church, the rectory, and the convent of the Sisters of Charity all to the ground. They marched south toward Philadelphia proper. They passed a German Catholic Church along the way and left it without incident, but when they got to the Irish Catholic Church of Saint Augustine's in Philadelphia, the mob again went wild. Saint Augustine's was left in smoldering ruins.

As the battle moved into center city, the rich and politically powerful found that they had no stomach for this type of activity in their own backyard. The militia was called out in full force. Martial law was declared and churches were guarded.

The Catholic leaders of the community called for their parishioners to cease all violence. Bishop Francis Kenrick arranged for all church services to be canceled. His noble appeal called for calm, claiming that it was better to have all the churches burned than to shed one drop of blood. He asked that the Catholics wait for the justice system to work.

Unfortunately the justice system failed the Catholics. The non-Irish/non-Catholic juries found no fault among the American Republicans, yet they convicted all the Irish involved. Tensions continued to ride high.

By July other Catholic churches in Philadelphia were being threatened. Saint Philip Neri Church in Southwark was a target for many of these threats. Members of this parish got permission to arm themselves in defense. While this may seem a reasonable attitude to take, it was in fact disastrous. On July 6, Republicans marched to Southwark. The official government militia was there to protect the church, but they were forced aside. When the Republicans had the temerity to shoot on the parish members guarding the church, the Catholics shot back. The mob had even acquired three cannon from the docks and shot those at the militia as well. This time the mob was bent on extreme destruction. The windows of the church were shattered and then they moved inside and methodically destroyed the contents of the church. They finished the job by burning Saint Philip Neri Church to the ground.

The violence in July was greater than the May incident at the market. Five thousand militiamen were called in to quell the riot. Fifteen lives were lost and at least fifty more people were injured.

This was a very sad chapter in Philadelphia history. The Irish immigrants never got any satisfaction from the government for these misdeeds. Over time, the Irish were assimilated into American culture. Proud Irish Americans serve in every aspect of American and Philadelphian government and society today.

THE SAD FATE OF THE
SWIMMING ELEPHANTS

- 1847 -

VIRGINIA AND PIZARRO, TWO FULL-GROWN MALE ELEPHANTS, were the property of Messrs. Raymond & Company of the Zoological Institute. A menagerie (worth a grand sum of thirty thousand dollars) including Virginia and Pizarro was to be transported from Philadelphia across the Delaware River to Camden, New Jersey. Research turns up no specific details as to why they were being transported, but it may safely be assumed that a display or show of the animals had been arranged in that community.

On Thursday, April 15, 1847, a ferry was arranged to move the beasts across the river. Numerous attempts were made to coax Virginia and Pizarro down the ferry slip. It had been determined that the heavy planks of the ferry slip would be durable enough to support such a massive load, but the elephants seemed to have a differing opinion. Their keeper, Mr. Nutter, used all his wiles to convince the elephants to (you should pardon the expression) "walk the plank."

However, when something the size of an elephant won't obey commands, there isn't much chance of changing its mind.

Mr. Nutter proposed an alternate plan—to swim the animals across the Delaware. Mammals in general are natural-born swimmers, and elephants are no exception. Tireless swimmers aided by their large bulk and the constant motion of their four legs, elephants swim with only the top of their heads protruding from the water and their trunks above the water acting as a natural snorkel. Scientists and historians believe that elephants swam from India to Sri Lanka to settle and prosper on that island, so their short trip across the Delaware River should have been a quick jaunt for these two elephants.

Mr. Nutter led his charges to the Marine Railway Southwark to see if that might appeal to Virginia and Pizarro. The elephants cooperated fully in this endeavor and without delay took the plunge. It seemed that not even the cold water put a damper on their playful dip.

It must be pointed out that the first major gaffe occurred before the elephants entered the water. The elephants had been yoked together for the journey—apparently it was easier to control the two giants in that manner, as one needed to convince only a single partner to progress on a desired path and the other would follow of necessity—and the yoke was not removed before their swim.

As the elephants progressed across the river, the tireless Mr. Nutter accompanied the swimmers in a small skiff. All proceeded to plan until the group reached mid-stream. There was a strong current and the elephants found it difficult to fight. Nonplussed, they simply turned with the current and proceeded in a fashion that would take them a couple of miles off target.

Virginia was the first to falter. It is not known what caused his distress, but soon his efforts began to fail and after two or three complete dunkings, he sank. Mr. Nutter was wild with consternation. He pulled alongside the animals and made a very valiant attempt to grapple the yoke with a long hooked spear. Pizarro grabbed the hook with his mouth and, between Nutter's urgent pulling and the elephants' desperate hold, the hook disengaged from the pole. That was pretty much the end of the fight. Perhaps the yoke was in some fashion responsible for Virginia's problems, but it was the deciding factor for Pizarro. Without the yoke it is likely that Pizarro could have completed his journey, but Pizarro could not maintain the swim while being pulled under by Virginia's waterlogged mass. Pizarro's trunk finally disappeared below the water line.

The *Daily Mercury* newspaper account stated, "They seemed conscious of their situation—their inevitable fate—and their last looks toward their keeper were of regret and agony, as if sorrowing to leave him."

A MAN INVENTS HIS KILLER

- 1867 -

WILLIAM BULLOCK WAS A MULTITALENTED MAN. He was a very gifted inventor, with a special ability to tinker with existing machinery and make it more efficient. Through the course of his career, he designed a number of machines for the agricultural community, including a cotton and hay press and a mechanical seed planter.

When he was still in his twenties, Bullock invented a shingle cutter that quickly and cleanly cut roofing shingles. It was so revolutionary that young William decided to go into the manufacturing business for himself, but that business did not do well and he moved on.

Bullock then invented a lathe-cutting machine, but it was his next invention, a grain drill, that brought him his first recognition, and in 1849 the Franklin Institute in Philadelphia honored him.

By this point in his life William Bullock had married, fathered seven children, been widowed, and remarried. He and his second wife would have six more children. While his inventions had brought him notoriety, they had not made him rich. So Bullock started a new career in Philadelphia as a newspaper editor for the *Banner of the Union.* It was this move that led to his most important contribution to the worlds of machinery and printing.

Bullock turned his inventive eye to the printing press. Back in the 1840s, inventor Richard Hoe improved on the original printing press. Hoe's rotary design greatly increased the speed with which newspapers could be printed. The next big obstacle for printing machines was to delete the laborious task of hand-feeding sheets of paper.

William Bullock achieved that standard and much, much more. Over the course of several years, he perfected the web rotary press. This amazing machine was designed to feed giant rolls of paper through the press. It also allowed the paper to be printed on both sides simultaneously. Furthermore the press was self-adjusting and had the capability to fold the paper, thus eliminating another labor-intensive task. The final stage of this miraculous invention involved a sharp serrated blade that precisely cut the paper to a uniform length. Bullock's astounding machine could print twelve thousand sheets per hour. After a couple of years of tinkering, he improved that number to thirty thousand sheets per hour.

Bullock's last invention would finally lead to the fame and fortune that he had strived for his entire life. At the age of fifty-four, Bullock was back in Philadelphia installing one of his popular machines. This unit was being set up for the *Philadelphia Ledger* newspaper, and Bullock took a real hands-on approach to his machinery. The installation process for a complicated piece of equipment could take weeks. It was also important to him to stick around and make sure everything was functioning properly. Bullock additionally used this time to look for ways to improve his invention.

On April 3, 1867, the inventor was fiddling with his machine. A driving belt had become detached from a pulley. The proper thing to do in a situation such as this would be to shut off the machine and reinstall the belt. Maybe Bullock had something pressing on his mind. Maybe he was just in a hurry. Whatever the case, he made a fatal mistake: He attempted to jam the belt back onto the pulley by means of a sharp kick with his foot while the machine was running full bore. Having worked with machinery his whole life, he probably recognized his error almost immediately. His foot and then his lower leg were quickly entangled in the machine. Help came quickly, but not soon enough. The machine was shut down, but the damage was done. William Bullock's leg and foot were mangled beyond hope.

He was rushed to the hospital, where a second mistake was made. The doctors should have amputated his leg right then, but instead they made an attempt to save the limb. Within a few days gangrene infected the leg. Finally, on April 12, 1867, the doctors attempted to cut off the appendage, but unfortunately Bullock died during the operation.

William Bullock will live forever in history. His accomplishments and inventions, especially the web rotary press, ensure his continued memory. Sadly, he will also be remembered as one of the few successful inventors that built the machine that killed him.

THE AUTOPSY OF CHANG AND ENG

- 1874 -

THE DEATHS OF CHANG AND ENG BUNKER on January 17, 1874, brought to an end two amazing lives. Even after their deaths, the original "Siamese Twins" were able to do one more thing for society at large: Their bodies were brought from their home in Mt. Airy, North Carolina, to the Mutter Museum of the College of Physicians in Philadelphia. It was here that the best medical minds of the time were able to study the phenomenon of the Siamese Twins with an eye to improving the human condition. It was only fitting that Chang and Eng could provide this service, as their remarkable lives had contributed so much already.

This story has its start sixty-three years earlier and as far away from Philadelphia as one can get while remaining on the same planet. On May 11, 1811, a woman named Nok gave birth to twins in the village of Meklong in the country of Siam (present-day Thailand). The boys were delivered together in a single birth of a sort of "yin and yang ball." Both children were healthy as evidenced by their cries. It was not until they were pried apart that the attending midwives realized they were physically connected by a short, fleshy, cartilage ligament just below the breastbone. Other than that they were as normal as any healthy newborns.

Poor, uneducated farmers and fishermen of the village were appalled and even believed it may have been the work of evil. Some believed the boys should be put to death. Many believed the birth signaled the end of the world. Word of the strange twins spread far and wide. Doctors were of the opinion that they should be separated despite the belief that this procedure would cause their deaths. The ruler of Siam, King Rama II, decided that in order to divert disaster Chang and Eng should be put to death.

Nok managed to keep everyone away from her youngest children. As time passed and no great calamity struck, the matter was forgotten. Chang and Eng were able to grow. Nok did not pamper her twins—they learned to walk, swim, and do chores like their siblings. At the age of eight the boys lost their father and five siblings to a cholera epidemic that savaged their village.

Now the young conjoined twins were needed to help the remaining family financially and they did so to good effect. They tried their hands at fishing like their father before them and became small-time merchants. In short they grew up very fast, learning to fend for themselves in a hard world. But the boys were extremely well liked, inquisitive, and well rounded.

By the age of fourteen they came to the attention of the new ruler of Siam, Rama III, and were invited to the palace in the capital city of Bangkok. Just a few years later their celebrity grew to the point that Westerners in the area took notice. By their eighteenth birthday they were on a ship to the United States of America. Essentially they had been bought from their mother for the express purpose of being displayed for money.

This was not a disagreeable situation. Nok and the twins were compensated, and in the bargain the teenagers got the opportunity to see the world. After stops in Boston, Providence, and New York, Chang and Eng made their first visit to the City of Brotherly Love. By the time they got to Philadelphia they already had an "act" that involved athletic tumbling and maneuvers. Their command of the English language was impressive and their amazing coordination wowed audiences everywhere.

They went on to tour America and Europe and somehow managed to settle down on a farm in Mt. Airy, North Carolina. It was here at the age of thirty-two that the boys met, wooed, and married a pair of sisters. These unions produced a total of twenty-one offspring. It can be left to the imagination how this feat was accomplished.

During these years the brothers were successful farmers and upstanding members of their community. That coupled with their occasional tours kept them and their families in a very comfortable lifestyle. All through their lives doctors from all over the world told them that surgical separation would most likely end in their deaths. The brothers also believed that when one died the other would die as well.

This premonition came true in January of 1874. Chang had been ill for a couple of days. Eng woke up in the night to discover his brother had died. The family physician, Dr. Hollingsworth, was sent for immediately, but by the time he arrived Eng was gone, too. Sadly, Hollingsworth believed that in the event of one twin's demise, the other could be saved with quick and radical surgery.

It was to find answers to the question of whether one life could be saved that Hollingsworth convinced the bereaved widows to send their husbands' remains to Philadelphia. In 1874 Philadelphia could boast some of the finest doctors in the world. The College of Physicians would be very excited to find out what made Chang and Eng tick.

Many questions were left unanswered at this point. While Chang had been sick, Eng had shown no signs whatever of illness. Quite the opposite, Eng seemed to be in the pink of health. Was it possible that Eng died of fright, or could his life have drained from his body through the ligament to his dead brother? Perhaps the sickness from Chang had passed through the connection to claim Eng.

The lead force in preparing for this autopsy was Dr. William H. Pancoast. He was a professor of general, descriptive, and surgical anatomy at the Jefferson Medical College in Philadelphia. His hope was that a medical examination of the connecting band of the brothers would help determine if the twins could have been successfully separated in life.

When the specially made casket containing the remains of Chang and Eng arrived at the Mutter Museum, little time was wasted. Dr. Pancoast directed the official autopsy. Eight days of inspections, incisions, and carefully noted observations led up to the official report presented to leading medical professors and surgeons in the Hall of the College of Physicians. The bottom line of their findings was that the twins could not have been separated in life without at least one, and probably both, of the brothers dying.

Dr. Pancoast and Dr. Harrison Allen were in agreement as to cause of death. They felt that Chang had died of a cerebral clot. Allen further stated that Eng's death was caused by sheer fright. Pancoast could neither confirm nor disprove that theory. He felt the post mortem was inconclusive on this point. A third physician, Dr. Summerall, put forward a different theory as to Eng's demise. He attempted to show that Chang's death and subsequent heart failure put such a strain on Eng's heart to continue pumping blood to his brother that it brought about his own death. No firm agreement was reached on this point.

Probably the most important information to come from the autopsy was medical knowledge of conjoined twins and a better understanding of the mysterious workings of the human body. With today's superior medical knowledge, it is known for a fact that the twins could have been successfully separated. It would now be a simple operation with a virtually 100 percent survival rate. Plaster casts of Chang and Eng, as well as photographs of them, are on display to this day at the Mutter Museum.

THE GREAT EXPOSITION

- 1876 -

WHEN SOMETHING HAS BEEN AROUND FOR one hundred years, it deserves a party. Philadelphia was the natural choice of location to hold this event considering the country started here and Philadelphia was not going to let the country down. Philadelphia was going to show the world what a one-hundred-year celebration should look like. The party started May 10, 1876, and ran all the way past dark the night of November 9 the same year. Anybody who was anybody attended . . . and so did almost everyone else!

This most spectacular event in Philadelphia history came to be known as the Centennial Exposition, but the official name was actually the "International Exhibition of Arts, Manufactures and Products of the Soil and Mine." This convoluted title was chosen to describe what became the most successful World's Fair to that date, in terms of extravagance and attendance.

An event of this magnitude could never be fully described in a mere chapter of this small book. The importance of the many inventions, innovations, and contributions in the fields of art, science, agriculture, and education are so numerous and varied that a number of volumes have been dedicated to that task. This is an outline of the highlights and pertinent details of an event that led the United States into a position of prominence in the world as an industrial power and cultural leader.

More than ten years of planning and eleven million dollars were poured into this project. The first decision the Centennial organizers made was an easy one . . . location. Beautiful Fairmount Park was chosen for a host of reasons. The park provided excellent access to the public. The grounds were magnificently manicured and spacious enough to accommodate the many buildings needed to house exhibits, restaurants, theaters, and services. The planners learned of the importance of these factors and others by studying the problems incurred by other cities that had held World's Fairs. This planning paid off: Philadelphia's fair was a commercial and practical success.

The Exposition was incredibly large. There were some thirty thousand exhibitors over the course of the six-month run. There were six main exhibition buildings including the Main Hall, which enclosed twenty-one and a half acres and was the largest building in the world at that time. There were also in excess of two hundred and fifty other smaller buildings and pavilions. The Exposition even boasted its own hospital that provided free medical care to all attendees. A separate water system was created to prevent any outbreak of disease. It is easy to see why planning and logistics were so important.

The unquestioned star of the fair was Machinery Hall. Most visitors made this technological wonder their first stop. The vast majority of the guests had never seen an electric light, let alone an elevator that was powered by the humongous Corliss steam engine. The fourteen hundred horsepower Corliss provided all the electrical power needed for the entire fair. These visitors had likely heard of these magical machines, but the newest technologies were undoubtedly an overwhelming surprise. Machinery Hall provided the first real glimpse into the future with working models of typewriters, mechanical calculators, Thomas Edison's newfangled telegraph, and a brand-new invention displayed by a Scottish immigrant whose name rings a bell.

Alexander Graham Bell showed off his new "telephone." This device had just been patented in March of the same year. The amazing machine allowed an individual to actually speak to and hear another individual instantaneously even if great distances separated the two. Today this feat is taken for granted, but imagine being a merchant in New York that has a regular need to amend an order from a supplier in Philadelphia. One quick phone call could add the goods to that shipment instantly. The possibilities were endless.

This fair was not just about the future; it also encompassed the past. One prominent and well-visited display was Benjamin Franklin's printing press. An entire colonial village was constructed and the Agricultural Hall displayed colonial farming techniques alongside the modern tools of that profession. While the newest sewing machines were strutting their stuff in the Machinery Hall, old-time looms and spinning wheels decorated the Women's Pavilion.

Entire buildings were devoted to individual states and foreign countries. Dignitaries, politicians, and celebrities hobnobbed with commoners in every corner of the exposition. Famous works of art including paintings and sculptures adorned every building and music concerts took place daily. All of this entertainment, adventure, and excitement were available to the public for the fifty-cent price of admission.

A total of 8,004,325 paid admissions were collected for the fair and the total admissions were a staggering 9,789,392. Many of course visited more than once. The greatest attendance in a single day was recorded on Thursday, September 28, which was appropriately "Pennsylvania Day," when a total of 257,286 people visited the fair.

One event that took place during the fair stands out historically. On July 4, 1876, five women slipped through the crowd toward the speaker's platform. The gathering was large on this holiday and few people took notice of the infiltrators. Nor were they aware that these women were on a mission.

These women were not invited to participate in the ceremonies that day; in fact their request to make a presentation was politely denied by the men in charge of the festivities. However these were women that were not easily deterred. The leader of the group was Susan B. Anthony. She and her four colleagues, Matilda Gage, Sara Spencer, Lillie Blake, and Phoebe Couzins, were all members of the newly formed Women's Suffrage Association.

Each of the women had secured for the day the coveted passes that designated them as members of the press. The five deftly slid through the crowd. There was only a small protest as the ladies joined the all-male press corps. Eyebrows were raised at the sight of these female reporters. The brief diversion was soon ignored as people's attention turned back to the podium and the many dignitaries that were scheduled to speak.

The foreign luminaries in attendance included Dom Pedro, the Emperor of Brazil; Prince Oscar of Sweden; and Count Rochambeau of France. The fact that these men and many big shots from the United States were here meant that security would be tight. The women were not fools. They had little hope that they would be able to disrupt these proceedings.

Their plan was a simple one. They brought with them many copies of their organization's new Declaration of Women's Rights and intended to distribute as many of the pamphlets as possible to the throngs. The hope was that they might create any sort of diversion that could bring attention to their cause. Meanwhile the ladies patiently waited in the press box for any opening that might be exploited.

Much of the audience that day was looking forward to the reading of the original Declaration of Independence by Richard Henry Lee. His performance was electrifying. The response from the crowd was boisterous to say the least; they were so wild and enthusiastic that few even noticed the band playing the national anthem of Brazil in tribute to Dom Pedro.

Susan B. Anthony recognized this golden opportunity and quickly made her move. Slipping onto the stage she approached the podium, which was currently manned by none other than the vice president of the United States, Thomas W. Ferry. Ironically it was this very same gentleman who had refused Ms. Anthony's request to speak on this platform. She offered a pamphlet to Ferry, who decidedly refused. Ferry called for security to remove the invader.

She wasted no time, using the confusion of the moment to read the beginning of the Women's Declaration. Security interrupted her rendition, but the damage, so to speak, had already been done. The four accomplices were hurriedly passing out copies to all as they fled down the aisles. Eager hands grabbed for the free information. All in all there was quite a ruckus.

And that is how Susan B. Anthony and her band of renegades got the second Declaration of Independence entered into the record at the Great Exposition of 1876.

November 9 marked the closing of the celebration, topped off with fireworks. The entire Exposition was such a complete success that other cities attempted to copy the event, but most met with just moderate success or outright failure.

The Centennial Celebration in Philadelphia was more than just a great big birthday party. It was a sign to the entire world that the United States of America had the class of a much more mature nation and could stand among the greatest countries and be considered equals in culture, science, and industry.

A RUNAWAY KID

- 1892 -

HIS GIVEN NAME WAS WILLIAM CLAUDE, and his parents chose to call him Claude. Even as a boy he hated the name. He preferred to be called Whitey and encouraged everybody to call him by that name. The nickname came honestly: Whitey was fair-skinned with light blond, almost white hair. Whitey was a tough kid. He wasn't a big kid, but he was known to be a real scrapper. The bigger and tougher neighborhood bullies doled out a fair share of beatings to the boy, but Whitey never backed down. He gained quite a reputation and earned a certain amount of respect from his peers.

Whitey's family history helps paint the picture of his boyhood. His father, Jim, was an immigrant from England. Jim was only a couple generations removed from minor royalty in Great Britain. His great-grandfather was a Lord, but the title and lands ended up with a family member who was a clergyman. In short, nothing passed down to Jim. Jim didn't exactly find the American Dream in Philadelphia, either, but he usually had a job of one kind or another. Jim was "fond of the bottle," as they say, and very quick of temper.

While these explosions were often violent and scary, they were usually short-lived.

Whitey's mother, Kate, had a well-known sense of humor. It has been said that she was sarcastic and would often stand at her front door greeting neighbors with pleasantries as they passed. When the neighbor was out of earshot, she would make snide humorous asides at his or her expense. Kate was a large woman and a bit lazy about housework but very shrewd with a dollar. She managed her household, her husband, and her five children all on an inconsistent and meager income. Whitey, or Claude as she called him, was Kate's first-born.

Jim had different jobs during Whitey's youth, including bartender and trolley operator. By the time Whitey was old enough to start helping with the family's income, Jim was running a food cart. He hawked his wares, which consisted mostly of fruits and vegetables, in the streets. At about age nine, Whitey's duties included running deliveries to upper-floor apartments and drumming up business by yelling out the names of the products available that day.

Whitey did not respond well to authority. His early life was a constant struggle with his parents and his father in particular. Whitey did attend school; however he did not find the authority there any more acceptable than that of his own family. There is some question as to how much formal schooling he completed, but it certainly was sporadic and largely unsuccessful. On the other hand, he was always very clever and did a surprising amount of reading on his own.

As Jim and his son worked side by side on the food cart, their disagreements grew more frequent and more volatile. Whitey had been to a vaudeville show and became enamored with jugglers. He would often attempt to replicate juggling feats using his father's produce. Needless to say this did not sit well with Dad, since bruised fruit is difficult if not impossible to sell. Whitey did not let the regular cuffing and smacks from his father deter his attempts to learn this fascinating new craft. It seems these two could not find neutral ground in any arena.

While this family battle escalated over the next few years, the father and son became more violent with each other. Things came to a head in the spring of 1892. Different versions of the story exist, but this is the most likely sequence of events. It seems Jim was walking through the yard when he stepped on a small shovel, which flipped up and hurt him. Whitey witnessed this action and apparently found a little too much humor in his father's pain. Dad proceeded to throw the offending shovel at his son. Whitey, having also reached a breaking point with his violent father, struck back with a peach basket to the noggin.

Whitey immediately realized that he had crossed a dangerous line and lit out as fast as his young legs could carry him. Jim recovered quickly and took up the chase. As he sprinted after the boy, he yelled about the consequences that awaited his son if he ever dared to return. Whitey had no such intentions. He didn't just run away; he was now officially homeless. He knew he could not go back.

Whitey was pretty well liked by his contemporaries in spite of his bullying ways. Older boys in particular took to the young ruffian. They were tough guys too and they respected a kid who could take a beating and come back to stand his ground. These friends came in handy for the young homeless boy. His first shelter was a simple hole in the ground covered by wood. This bleak domicile was furnished only with an old blanket for comfort. Fortunately for Whitey, that spring was mild and the weather allowed this setup to be acceptable. Friends would bring food stolen from home. The other young toughs held a good bit of admiration for the youngster that defied the authorities and the odds. The young rebel was living their own dreams of independence.

Regrettably the good weather did not last very long. Rain turned the dirt hole into a freezing mud bath. To make matters worse,

Whitey's friends began to get caught at their petty grocery larcenies, which dried up the all-important food supply. Whitey took to scrounging for stables and open cellars for shelter, and he began a life of crime to feed himself. He would snatch an apple from a cart or sneak into a bar to gorge on the free lunch. This was just the beginning of a life that would be associated with both saloons and their beverages. He spent close to a year on the streets and became well known to the police and hobos alike.

Over the next couple of years, Whitey spent time with his maternal grandmother, an uncle, friends, and total strangers. There was some schooling and a variety of odd jobs. One constant through all this was the juggling. He kept at it and improved dramatically. There was no question that he had a natural ability. In fact Whitey went on to make a career in show business, starting out as a simple juggler. From the start of his career he was always funny. His humor soon eclipsed his juggling skills. Many consider him the most unique comedian of his time. He became a major star in vaudeville, movies, and on the radio. Whitey's full name at birth was William Claude Dukenfield, but he is best remembered by his shortened stage name . . . W. C. Fields.

It is true that Fields had quite a bit of fun at Philadelphia's expense over the years, which can probably be attributed to a very rough childhood in that city. One of his most remembered remarks concerned prizes in a contest, where he said first prize was a one-week vacation in Philadelphia; second prize was two weeks. There is no truth to the legend concerning his headstone, however, which is widely rumored to read, "I'd rather be here than in Philadelphia." There are two things that go without question: William Claude Dukenfield was one of the funniest and best-loved comedians and curmudgeons of all time, and he remains one of Philadelphia's favorite sons.

MUMMER'S PARADE

- 1901 -

TUESDAY, JANUARY 1, 1901, USHERED IN A NEW YEAR, a new decade, and a new century. This very special day was celebrated like no other day in Philadelphia's storied history. There had been Mummer's Parades and Shooter's Parades on the streets of Philadelphia on many New Year's Days, but this was the consolidation that brought all the varied groups in the city together once and for all.

Prior to 1901 many different ethnic groups and organizations held either Mummer's Parades or Shooter's Parades. These various assemblies traveled different routes through South Philadelphia, often colliding with one another and creating all kinds of havoc. Members of one neighborhood or ethnic group would fight with anyone bold enough to cross their turf or interrupt their celebration. As of 1901 the "pig men" brought all that chaos to an end.

What is a "Mummer," anyway? Well, the tradition dates back to medieval Europe, where masked and costumed men and women paraded during festivals such as Christmas and Saturnalia. Nothing quite so grand led to Philadelphia's indoctrination of this event, however. In the New World the Mummers had a more sedate beginning.

There are records of young men wandering the streets during the week between Christmas and New Year's Day all the way back before the 1700s. Sometimes they would be masked and always they were rowdy. In fact it was not uncommon to set off firecrackers or even shoot guns to greet the New Year. Sometimes these pranksters would sing or recite a poem in the hopes of being rewarded with a cookie, some cake, or something to drink.

As South Philadelphia began to develop and expand it became a true melting pot: Irish, Jews, Italians, African Americans, Poles, and others settled into an unusual community. Each of these groups naturally brought with them their own customs, and each of these groups developed their own versions of this celebration. By the mid 1800s there were competitions with prizes for costumes, music, and comedy. There was also confusion, as one group's celebration would often spill over into the next neighborhood. As time passed these conflicts became more pronounced and the resulting friction required more and more police involvement. This did not escape the notice of local government.

Attempts to consolidate the parades failed year after year, until the "pig men" got involved. The "pig men" were actually the Vare brothers, also known as "The Slop-cart Statesmen." These three brothers—George, Edmund, and William—were born and raised in South Philadelphia on a pig farm.

All three brothers were involved in the garbage business, collecting slop to feed their pigs. As they prospered they went into other business ventures, including construction and ultimately, politics—the arena in which they excelled. There is sufficient evidence to portray them as fairly corrupt but also very astute politicians. Often they would refuse salaries for their elected offices and instead funnel those monies into local charities to win the public to their side. The overall effect was to create a mini-empire that held control of the city for many years.

One very positive accomplishment of the Vare brothers was to consolidate the various ethnic Mummers into one huge but manageable parade. They designated Broad Street—then the longest continuous street in the nation—for the course of the parade. How did the brothers convince all these battling factions to band together? The answer is the oldest in the book: Large cash prizes did the trick.

As the fog from New Year's Eve lifted, many different groups and associations converged on the intersection of Reed and Broad Streets in South Philly. The parade route would follow Broad Street north through the center of town all the way to Girard Avenue. The brisk winter day did nothing to deter the crowds. This parade had been extensively advertised and people came from miles around to line the parade route. Despite the holiday, ferries from New Jersey ran constantly to bring the throngs of spectators into the city.

In the center of town a reviewing stand was constructed. It included a temporary hut to house the judges. Many public buildings were opened downtown so dignitaries who were unable to cram into the stands could watch the show from indoors.

At precisely 10 a.m. the first of the Mummers began the long march up Broad Street, following a contingent of Philadelphia's proud horse-mounted policemen. At approximately 10:30 the procession made its way to the reviewing stand. As each of the various clubs and organizations reached this pivotal "center stage," their members would commence with their planned entertainment for the judges' review.

There are varying accounts as to the total number of clubs participating that day. Twenty-three different organizations were listed in the following day's newspapers. The clubs also varied in size from twenty members to more than three hundred. The contest was divided into two distinct groups, called the Fancy Dressed Clubs and the Comic Clubs.

The Fancy Dressed Clubs were easy to distinguish from their Comic counterparts. The Fancy Dressers portrayed kings and knights, pirates and tribal leaders. Their costumes were colorful and designed using silks, satins, and other fine cloth. The costumes were also extravagant. A king's train might be twenty feet long, with many accompanying pages to keep the royal robe from touching the ground. There were very few women in the parade, but some men dressed as women to represent female royalty.

All the clubs traveled with their own music and instruments. The African-American clubs were bedecked in feathers and colorful scarves and were not alone in favoring jazz music. There were many string bands featuring banjos and brass bands, and almost every club featured singers. American Indians were represented as well as Chinese, Irish, Jews, Italians, and Poles.

The Comic Clubs showed an inventiveness that would rival the great parades of today. While the Comics also had music, that was about all they shared with the Fancies. The Comics created wonderful conveyances that included carts and mules, chariots and horses, and manually powered imitations of automobiles. Their costumes ran the gamut from matching outlandish uniforms to rags patched together with more rags.

The competition for prizes was fierce and the judges would be faced with difficult decisions. Nearly two full hours of entertainment and spectacle was presented to them at the reviewing stand. The judges had to make their determinations based on entertainment value, outrageousness, musical accomplishment, quality and beauty of costumes, inventiveness, and of course the most important facet of the Comics . . . humor.

The Fancy Dressed Clubs was the smaller of the two categories.

There were four prizes awarded in this class. The first prize of three hundred dollars was awarded to the Elkton Association, which was captained by George W. Waitmann. The Elkton group was composed of 250 members, so each teammate netted a little over one dollar in prize money. The second-place prize went to the George A. Furnival Association, whose 250 members shared two hundred fifty dollars. The Silver Crown New Year Association placed third. The one hundred fifty dollar-prize made this organization the most financially successful of the Fancies, as there were only fifty members sharing the pot. Fourth place went to the John F. Slater Association captained by John Broomley, with 250 members splitting one hundred dollars.

There were by far many more entries in the Comic category. This class had six prizes and much more colorful club names. A short list of the losers includes the Hardly Ables, the Doodlebachs, the Early Risers, the White Turnips, and the Half and Halfs.

The Comic first prize of three hundred dollars was given to the White Cap Association, headed by George A. Albertson and consisting of only forty members. That came to a princely $7.50 each! The Daniel Duane Association and its team of twenty nabbed second place and two hundred fifty dollars. At $12.50 per teammate they must be considered the overall winners.

All of the newspaper critics agreed that the real winners were the spectators. The reviews of all the performers were top-notch. No estimates were made of the total crowd, but it is believed that it was the largest the city had ever seen.

The 1901 event was alternately referred to as both the Shooter's Parade and the Mummer's Parade. The reason for this was simple: Previous New Year's Day parades in Philadelphia had gone by both names. The Shooters got their name because they often shot guns into the air as noisemakers. While that unsafe practice had diminished by 1901, it had not disappeared. On January 2, the *Philadelphia Bulletin* newspaper reported an incident that involved a man firing his pistol as part of the New Year's celebration: Twenty-two-year-old William Smith accidentally shot a young woman named Lizzie Cox in the arm. It is most likely that unacceptable episodes such as this are what led to the parade being more closely associated with King Momus who has come to be known as the face of the Mummers.

A final bonus for the city was the revenue raised by local merchants. Food booths flourished in the party atmosphere. The "pig men" struck gold for their city and an annual event was born that lasts to this day. So make plans to visit the Mummer's Museum, a favorite tourist stop in downtown Philadelphia, and to witness the Mummer's Parade in person. Bring the family, bring a sense of humor, and show up early to get a good seat.

Oh, and why not memorize the words to James Bland's "Oh, Dem Golden Slippers," now the traditional theme song of the Mummer's Parade? Bland wrote many songs in his career, including "Carry Me Back to Old Virginny," the state song of Virginia. His "Golden Slippers" is the one standard you can count on at the Mummer's Parade. It's fitting that Bland wrote this song, since he was a true mix of different cultures—African American, Native American, and Caucasian—just like the Mummer's Parade.

> *Oh, dem golden slippers! Oh, dem golden slippers!*
> *Golden slippers I'm gwine to wear*
> *Because they look so neat;*
> *Oh, dem golden slippers! Oh, dem golden slippers!*
> *Golden slippers I'm gwine to wear*
> *To walk de golden street.*

Of course, that's to walk one very special golden street—Broad Street, Philadelphia!

A STICKY SITUATION

- 1928 -

IN THE LATE 1800S AND EARLY 1900S CHEWING GUM was big business. Not only was it tasty, it was considered healthful to chew gum. Something like nine out of ten doctors agreed that it was relaxing for your facial nerves and muscles. Competition among candy and gum companies was tough, and an edge was needed to survive in the industry. That fact, and a penchant to add some fun to chewing gum, led to the search for a gum base that could blow bubbles.

Philadelphia native Walter Diemer gets the credit for "inventing" bubble gum, although according to him, "it was an accident." Diemer was born in 1904. He grew up and attended high school in Philadelphia. As a young adult he found employment in his hometown at the Fleer Corporation. The Fleer family business was formally a flavoring extracts factory dating back to 1849. The company was a Philadelphia icon for over one hundred years. They began making chewing gum in 1895 and bubble gum in 1928, but they closed their doors in 1995. In the late 1920s Mr. Diemer was a

Now that the successful formula had been concocted, it was time to color it, wrap it, and ship it off to candy stores. Mr. Diemer directed the factory workers to make a huge batch of gum. However, no one had checked the inventory, and when it came time to add color to the confection there was only one choice in stock—pink. So pink it was, and to this day, pink it is. The first pieces of bubble gum were wrapped up like taffy and marketed as Dubble Bubble. On December 26, 1928, the Fleer Corporation's bubble gum was first tested at a small Philadelphia candy store.

Mr. Diemer hand-delivered the bubble gum to local stores. He demonstrated his bubble-blowing skills to entice storeowners to buy Dubble Bubble and retail it through their stores. That strategy worked, so from then on he took time to teach salesmen how to blow bubbles. Imagine grown men chomping, chewing, stretching the pink blob over their tongues and blowing big bubbles. Who could resist a sales pitch like that? Bubble gum quickly became one of the most popular penny-candy selections in the glass-encased counters of corner stores all across America.

A piece of bubble gum cost one penny back then. Even in the hard economic times of 1929, and on through the 1930s, a person could afford a penny's worth of enjoyment. People splurged on Dubble Bubble one cent at a time, making it a huge financial success for the Fleer Company. The creation of a Dubble Bubble comic strip folded around the gum inside the wrapper came in 1930. The comic featured the Dubble Bubble twins, Dub and Bub. In 1941 Dubble Bubble gum squares were issued as rations to soldiers serving in World War II. The familiar taste and comic antics of Dub and Bub brought a bit of boyhood pleasure to a war-torn grown-up world.

Although the comic characters Dub and Bub were rubbed out in 1950, a character named Pud replaced them. In 1968 Dubble Bubble printed its one-thousandth comic. Pud was entertaining bubble gum fans then just as he is today. Dubble Bubble has changed over the years; now it comes in barrel shapes or chewy squares, and became available as bubble gum balls in 1999. Choices of fruit flavorings with corresponding colors have also been added through the years, yet the all-time-favorite original recipe is still on the market. Dubble Bubble's winning color is pink and the preferred flavor is "bubblegum."

Soon after the invention of bubble gum, the work of accounting fell to other employees at Fleer Chewing Gum Company. Mr. Walter Diemer worked his way up to senior vice president and held that position until his retirement in 1970. After retiring he remained a member of the board of directors of Fleer Corporation for another ten years.

Walter Diemer died in 1998. Just a few years before his death he was quoted as saying, "It was an accident. I was doing something else and ended up with something with bubbles." Yes indeed, he was doing something else when he got called to tend a vat of chewing gum base. But from then on he worked hard to perfect a recipe—finally presenting to the world a sweet, tasty, chewable piece of bubble gum called Dubble Bubble.

Walter Diemer did not patent his invention of bubble gum back in 1928, and soon other candy and gum companies were making their own versions of bubble gum. He never received any royalties, but that didn't matter to Walter. The fun of bubble gum was reward enough. For him it was quite a joy to offer kids a hunk of bubble gum, tell them the story of his invention, and hold bubble-blowing contests. What was the prize for winning those contests? . . . More bubble gum, of course.

THE 1929 ATHLETICS

- 1929 -

THE YEAR 1929 WAS A PIVOTAL ONE in the United States of America. The Roaring Twenties were winding down and headed to a disastrous finish. Prohibition was still the law and gangsters flourished from coast to coast. In the world of professional baseball there was a clear-cut king . . . the New York Yankees. But just like the stock market, the Yankees were on track for a crash of their own that year.

Most baseball historians agree to this day that the 1927 Yankees were the greatest team to ever play the game. Is it possible that another team might be more qualified for this title? This is a story about baseball, but more importantly it is a story about revenge, hard work, planning, team spirit, life, and the vision of one very special man. It is the story of the 1929 Philadelphia Athletics.

Connie Mack was a baseball man. Baseball was in his blood. Born Cornelius MacGillicuddy during the Civil War, he shortened his name to Connie Mack as was a common practice in those days. Connie spent a lifetime in and around the game. He played as an amateur and a professional with distinction. Following his playing days, he moved quite naturally into the world of coaching, where he excelled from the beginning. This can be attributed to his vast knowledge of the game and extreme competitive spirit. With hard work, perseverance, and a little luck he managed to become a part owner and eventually majority owner of the Philadelphia Athletics Baseball Club.

Connie's success came quickly and by 1910 he had put together the first baseball dynasty. The A's, as they were known, won the World Series in 1910, 1911, and again in 1913 under his tutelage. The baseball world openly acknowledged Connie as the best in the business. When that team started to fade, Mack dismantled it and spent the next seven years losing at an unbridled pace. Although his teams of the early 1920s got back on track, many considered him too "old-fashioned" to compete in the new era of baseball.

The "new era" featured the likes of Babe Ruth and Lou Gehrig, and the fabulous New York Yankees owned them both. This was the era of the long ball and the home run was king. What few seemed to notice was that Connie Mack knew the game as well as anyone alive. He had been quietly scouting and building his own powerhouse team all through the twenties. In fact the A's had managed quite respectably in 1927 and 1928, finishing second to the Yankees in the American League race. While no one was picking them to upset the Yankees in 1929, they were actually more than just respectable. They were a very solid ball club on the verge of being great.

The young team's potential was evident even in spring training that year. Not only were the boys playing well, they were also playing loose and having fun. A look at the players themselves reveals a lot about the character of the team. Connie had put together a group of men with an amazing amount of talent. He looked for two things in a baseball player. The first quality was ability—Mack wanted big guys with athletic aptitude. The second quality that this masterful technician expected was smarts. He drafted his players from colleges rather than sandlots. As a result Connie Mack fielded a team that not only played well, they played smart. This was their edge.

The team was made up of many future Hall of Famers including Robert "Lefty" Grove, Mickey Cochrane, Eddie Collins, Al Simmons, and a very young future phenomenon by the name of Jimmie Foxx. All of the players had a zest for life and the game of baseball. They seemed to be happiest when they were playing the game. They also shared one more attribute: Both individually and as a team, they hated to lose. That bears repeating . . . they really hated to lose!

Lefty Grove is still considered one the best left-handed pitchers to ever climb the mound. When Lefty lost a game, it was not uncommon to find him in the clubhouse afterward wreaking havoc on anything that wasn't nailed down. He would throw anything he could lift and kick anything (or anyone) else. Mickey Cochrane was the uncontested field general of the team. While manning his position behind the plate, he was the heart and soul of the team. He also had the habit of throwing fits after a loss. Teammates reported that he would pull his hair, beat his head against a wall, and literally cry. It was said of Al Simmons that before he would step to the plate to face an opposing pitcher he would work himself up into a state of frenzied anger toward his opponent.

These are the kinds of traits that seemed to endear the players to their hometown fans. Philadelphia fans have always been fanatical. Yet a careful observation shows why these fans were especially drawn to these players. For one thing, the players mostly lived right in the same community as Shibe Park where the Athletics played their home games. These guys weren't just Philadelphians' team, they were their neighbors. And like the city they represented, these players were a diverse group ethnically. Cochrane, Foxx, and Mack were of Irish descent. There were Germans, Swedes, and Poles. In fact one of the stars, Al Simmons, was another of those to shorten his name; he was born Aloysius Szymanski. This was a group that the city of Philadelphia could embrace as its own.

The 1929 A's played great baseball all season. Under the guidance of Connie Mack, they fought all comers. No longer were there comments in the press about Connie being over the hill. This game most decidedly had not passed him by. On the contrary, he was at the forefront of his team. Connie set a perfect example for his players, the calm to their furious storm. Connie had the distinction of being the only coach who did not dress in uniform for the game. Instead, he could be found in the dugout decked out in his suit and tie. It is said the only days the jacket came off were the hottest of the summer. He was also a reverent man; he disdained the use of salty language and encouraged his players to do the same.

Mack was a religious man as well—if the team was home on a Sunday, you could find him at his Catholic church. The Blue Laws of that era prevented the playing of baseball on Sundays in Philadelphia, and despite his religious beliefs Connie was a foe of those laws. These laws were not observed in any other baseball town at the time, and as a businessman Connie felt the rules to be unfair to his organization.

The Blue Laws did not interfere with the quality of the team's play, however. As the season progressed, it became clear that the team to beat was the Philadelphia Athletics. The feared New York Yankees were not having a stellar year. The prodigious Babe Ruth was battling his own demons and the rest of that team was fighting just to stay in contention. The second-best team that year was the Washington Senators, led by the great Walter "The Train" Johnson.

The Senators gave the A's a run for their money, but in the waning days of the season the Philadelphia Athletics sealed the deal. The monster bats of Al Simmons and especially Jimmie Foxx were just too much for the competition. The A's were the pennant winners of the American League, earning the opportunity to face the Chicago Cubs of the National League in the World Series.

The World Series was a romp for the A's. Although Chicago had a very good team, they were simply no match for the powerful Athletics. Philadelphia prevailed by winning four games in their five meetings.

The Philadelphia Athletics went on to win the American League pennant in 1930 and 1931. They also won the World Series again in 1930 and just barely lost the '31 series to the St. Louis Cardinals by a margin of four to three. Thus Connie Mack, who was now referred to as the "Tall Tactician," created a second Philadelphia Athletics dynasty, getting his revenge on the New York Yankees and defending his name as a grand master in the art of baseball.

The A's franchise was sold to Kansas City in the 1950s and currently resides in Oakland, California. Not many of the old Philadelphia Athletics fans are left anymore, but the ones that are still around remember the team with pride. And if you want an argument over the greatest team ever, look one of these fans up. They will be happy to oblige.

MONOPOLY, A GAME OF BIG MONEY

- 1936 -

MONOPOLY IS THE ONE GAME THAT can be found in almost every American home. It is considered a valuable teaching tool that provides children and adults with lessons in the world of business and finance. The official story of the board game Monopoly states that Charles Darrow, an unemployed engineer, invented the game at his kitchen table in the Germantown section of Philadelphia. The truth is that Darrow did not invent the game, but he did create the version that has become one of the most successful games in the world.

The year 1930 dawned with the entire country engulfed in the beginning of the Great Depression. Charles Darrow was one of the victims of those difficult economic times. His former job as a salesman of engineering equipment was just one of the many casualties of the employment market. Like thousands of others Darrow was looking for work, and he filled his days with many different matters in an attempt to feed his family.

While searching for gainful employment, Darrow did a little

inventing and a lot of odd jobs, including walking dogs and fixing small electrical appliances. He devised a new bridge pad for the popular card game and created a beach toy that involved a ball and bat. This still left plenty of time for sitting at his kitchen table and doodling on the tablecloth. Those doodles centered on happier days spent with his family at their favorite vacation spot . . . Atlantic City, New Jersey.

This is where the official story might break with reality. Records and interviews indicate that Darrow and his wife were probably already familiar with a board game called the Landlord's Game, or at least a similar version of that game. The Landlord's Game was devised and patented in 1904 by a Quaker woman named Lizzie Magie. That game was actually more of a political statement and teaching tool that promoted the opposite of what the game Monopoly has come to portray. While Monopoly celebrates capitalism, the Landlord's Game had more of a communist flavor. Still, there were many similarities between the games. Magie's version also used street names, such as Easy Street and Poverty Place. The original also had the pieces moving around the outside part of the board and there were spaces for railroads, utilities, and good old "Go To Jail."

Back at the kitchen table in Germantown, Darrow was busy redesigning Magie's game into the one we know today. Darrow slowly transformed his tablecloth into his game board. Many attributes carried over from Magie's game. The utilities, various taxes, and jail spaces remained as before. All the street names were changed to reflect real Atlantic City locations. The railroad names corresponded to the actual rail lines that fed tourists into the seaside resort, though there are two discrepancies in the naming of rail lines. The Short Line is believed to refer to the Shore Fast Line, a streetcar line, and the B&O Railway did not have service to Atlantic City. If Darrow had done more research, he would have found that four rail lines did service Atlantic City in the 1930s—he missed the Jersey Central and the Seashore lines.

Only one street name from Darrow's original game was not an actual street in Atlantic City. That was Marvin Gardens. It is believed that Marvin Gardens refers to a housing project of the time located in neighboring Margate. That project's actual name was Marven Gardens.

As Charles worked on his design, he also played the game with family and friends. He quickly realized that he could make a small profit by hand-building more games, which he sold to friends for the princely sum of four dollars each. The game was very popular in his circle.

Money was so tight in the Darrow household that Charles resorted to any means available to manufacture these games. Playing pieces were colored buttons. Houses and hotels were carved out of scrap wood. Paint samples from a local hardware store added color to the board and all the deeds and play money were tediously made from scrap paper.

The time had come to look for help. The king of the board game business at that time was Parker Brothers. Charles Darrow sent a copy of his game, complete with rules, to be considered by the company. The response was not what Darrow wanted: Parker Brothers wrote that Monopoly had fifty-two separate design flaws. A couple of the company's objections were that the game took too long to play and the rules were too complicated.

Charles Darrow was stuck. Parker Brothers had turned him down, and he did not have the capital to manufacture the game in large quantities on his own. Yet his gut reaction was that he had a hit, and he decided it was time to take a risk. Darrow made an arrangement with a friend who had a printing business. The friend would supply the printing of deeds, cards, and play money while Darrow put together the boards, playing pieces, houses, and hotels.

The next step was to find outlets that would sell the product. Darrow convinced a few stores in Philadelphia to carry the game, and soon Darrow found himself working fourteen-hour days trying to keep up with demand, but it was a losing battle. Word spread quickly about this "new" board game. Historians believe that the sudden popularity was partially due to the Depression. Many people could not afford to go out to be entertained, and games played at home were an inexpensive alternative. Furthermore the excitement of playing with large sums of money, even fake money, held an appeal to the cash-starved masses.

It wasn't long before the game showed up on the shelves of F.A.O. Schwartz in New York City, the premier toy store in America. It was one of these games that ended up in the hands of a friend of Sally Barton. Sally was the daughter of George Parker, founder of Parker Brothers. Sally's friend raved about the game and suggested that Sally might want to tell someone at Parker Brothers about it. Sally went straight to the top of the company, probably during dinner—she was married to Robert Barton, the president of Parker Brothers.

Robert went out and purchased one of the hard-to-find games and played it that night. The very next day Robert Barton wrote a letter to Charles Darrow inviting him to a meeting about the game. This Parker Brothers encounter would have a very different ending than Darrow's last exchange with the company.

Charles Darrow made a deal that included a buyout of the game rights and a royalty on every game sold. The arrangement included some concessions. Parker Brothers wanted to ensure that the rules could be adapted to provide a short version of the game. Other more minor revisions were also included. The deal made Darrow a millionaire.

The Parker Brothers Company soon learned of Lizzie Magie's Landlord's Game as well as other versions that had sprouted from it.

In a very savvy business move the game company purchased all rights to those games, keeping the game of Monopoly safely in their hands ever since.

Charles Darrow retired at the age of forty-six and became a gentleman farmer with a penchant for world travel. A few years after his death, he was officially honored with a plaque on Atlantic City's Boardwalk, right near the intersection of Park Place.

ENIAC: THE FIRST ELECTRONIC
DIGITAL COMPUTER

- 1947 -

JOHN WILLIAM MAUCHLY WAS A YOUNG PHYSICS PROFESSOR at Ursinus College, just outside Philadelphia. His interest in high-speed calculating machines stemmed from his desire to predict weather more accurately. A thorough search of the existing calculating machines led him to believe that the mechanical machines of the day were woefully limited for his purposes. Mechanical computers and calculators were being researched heavily at both MIT and Harvard in Boston. Mauchly believed that electricity could somehow be used to calculate and he instinctively knew those little electrons would be thousands, maybe millions of times faster than anything mechanical. Nevertheless he traveled not only to Boston to investigate these machines, but also to Iowa, where John V. Atanasoff was working on an electronic device of his own. The Atanasoff contraption showed some real promise, but had severe limitations that made it impractical. It was also only in the design stage and there was no working model.

All of this research and information was boiling inside Mauchly's head in 1940 when he learned he had been accepted into an electronics course at the University of Pennsylvania's Moore School of Electrical Engineering. John Mauchly was the oldest student in the class and he was paired with the youngest man accepted into the course—John Adam Presper Eckert Jr., "Pres" to his friends, had just finished his bachelor's degree at Penn.

Pres Eckert was an engineer. There is no doubt he was born to that calling. In his youth he started tinkering with electrical devices and had a never-ending thirst for gadgets and gizmos. His passion was to take things apart and see if he could improve on the design.

Fittingly, both Mauchly and Eckert found the electronics course they were enrolled in to be simplistic and boring. However they discovered they shared similar desires and despite coming from different backgrounds and being different ages they became fast friends. They spent much of their time together discussing Mauchly's idea for an electronic calculator. Eckert thought that it would be difficult to manufacture, but not impossible. One of Eckert's great strengths was his ability to focus on a problem—like a dog with a bone he would not let go.

Mauchly was invited to join the Penn faculty as a physics professor, but it was a marriage of convenience more than a result of Penn's desire to have him. Mauchly was considered an odd bird and a dreamer, but the war was commandeering manpower and Mauchly was one of the few PhDs available to fill the teaching spot.

John Mauchly produced a seven-page proposal in August of 1942 entitled "The Use of High-Speed Vacuum Tube Devices for Calculation." His proposal was dismissed by the deans of Penn as the wild ramblings of a man known to be a radical dreamer, and the proposal was not even properly filed and saved.

Fortunately for the world of science, this same proposal did end up in the hands of Lieutenant Herman Goldstine. Goldstine was a mathematician with his own PhD who was drafted into the army. Goldstine knew that the army needed help with high-speed calculations for the firing tables of their new guns. He felt that this newfangled electronic computer might just be the tool to solve this tricky problem.

Mauchly had already enlisted Eckert as a vital part of the project. Goldstine loaded Mauchly and Eckert into the back of his Studebaker and headed to a meeting of the bigwigs at the Aberdeen Proving Grounds in Maryland. This was a risky move on Goldstine's part. The generals and colonels in the army of that era rarely showed interest in unproven technological advances. This was an incredibly radical and completely untested machine that Goldstine was proposing. His mission was to convince the army to come up with the funding.

A little good fortune was with Goldstine that day. These same officers had just been overridden on another fantastic scientific project. They had turned down the funding of the Manhattan Project, the program that would create a nuclear bomb. President Franklin Delano Roosevelt reversed their decision. It is a good bet that they did not want that to happen again.

The U.S. Army funded the contract for this machine, with a main purpose of determining firing solutions for new weapons being used in World War II. Essentially every new cannon or missile launcher needed huge amounts of mathematical calculations to determine where their respective projectiles would land. This information was vital so that the Army personnel could properly aim their weapons. The number of man-hours it took to make these calculations by hand was causing delays that were unacceptable to the war effort. Thus there was a need for a super-speedy "computing device."

Mauchly, Eckert, and Goldstine went back to the Moore School at Penn and began to assemble a team to build ENIAC (the acronym stands for electronic numerical integrator and computer). Time was of the essence. The war was raging in Europe, Africa, and the Pacific. The ENIAC team worked long hours and many men and women contributed important ideas toward the finished product. The main design, idea, and most of the work, however, was the pure inspiration of Eckert and Mauchly, who built the machine in Philadelphia. It took years of trial and error, not to mention many engineering changes, but the finished product exceeded even their wildest dreams.

ENIAC weighed over thirty tons and cost $486,804.22 when it was completed. It was comprised of thirty different units, plus a power supply and its own forced-air cooling device. This machine contained 17,468 vacuum tubes, 70,000 resistors, 10,000 capacitors, and approximately a half million soldered joints. Miles and miles of copper wiring allowed the "Giant Brain" to communicate with its various parts. ENIAC sucked 174 kilowatts of electricity. When ENIAC was not running a program, it consumed $650 per hour in electrical costs. As the project neared completion, both Eckert and Mauchly realized that they had made many errors in the design. Eckert in particular saw the potential improvements for future creations. A much smaller and more efficient computer was very feasible. Even before they were done, they began to design the second-generation computer. This is of course a pattern that continues to this day. Every time a new computer design leaves the drafting table it becomes obsolete due to new technologies.

As the scientific world became aware of the new technology, everyone wanted in on the action. Famous scientists such as the renowned mathematician John von Neumann became involved in the project. Von Neumann had some input into the design of the original ENIAC and he would later write a 101-page report outlining Mauchly and Eckert's design plans for the second generation known as EDVAC. Titled *First Draft of a Report on the EDVAC,* the paper was so well written that Goldstine sent it to many people in the scientific community—a rather surprising move considering this was a top-secret military matter. Suddenly people mistakenly believed the work of Mauchly and Eckert was really von Neumann's accomplishment.

The waters became murkier when Grist Brainerd from Penn began to realize that the harebrained scheme that he had vetoed from the start might actually be something big. When the army granted the funds to the University of Pennsylvania, Grist was put nominally in charge of the project. Now that it looked like it was bearing fruit, he tried to muscle in on the glory.

When the great brain ENIAC was finally shown to the world, it was an instant success. The demonstration took place in February 1946. Special programs were designed to show ENIAC's prowess. A series of light bulbs were connected to allow the spectators to "see" the machine in action. One of their computation examples was to have ENIAC multiply 13,975 by 13,975. The answer, 195,300,625, flashed up on the tote board in the blink of an eye. Finally ENIAC was fed an extremely complex problem that had taken experienced mathematicians a number of weeks to solve. This half-million-dollar machine spit out the correct answer in exactly fifteen seconds. The select audience of scientists, mathematicians, and VIPs was blown away by the presentation.

Unfortunately the machine wasn't completed until after the war was over. The good news was that this machine was still very valuable to the army. Because it was designed to handle any type of mathematical problems, it was also extremely useful in many other areas.

Mauchly and Eckert successfully patented their machine on June 26, 1947. The pair went on to start the very first electronic computer company with the idea that they would manufacture computers for business and governments. Sadly the inventors were not as good in business as they were at inventing. After years of struggle they were forced to sell their company to Remington Rand.

The Sperry Corporation purchased Remington Rand in 1955, and all through this time there were lawsuits going back and forth between IBM, Sperry, and other companies over the rights to manufacture computers.

After many court battles between these corporate giants, a judge in Minnesota determined that Mauchly and Eckert were not the inventors of the computer. The reason cited was that John V. Atanasoff (remember him from Iowa?) had the rudimentary idea before Mauchly. There is no doubt that Mauchly learned from Atanasoff, but the Mauchly/Eckert machine design was so different, so much better, that many believed it should be viewed as a separate invention. Additionally, Atanasoff never completed his inferior device. Most people familiar with the case believe that the judge was simply cleaning up the mess of lawsuits by putting everyone on even ground. In fact the only losers were Mauchly and Eckert.

Fame and fortune eluded this entrepreneurial pair of Philadelphia geniuses, but the truth is there to see: These men were the fathers of the computer generation.

A MIRACLE

- 1949 -

ON JULY 8, 1949, THE PARENTS OF J. Kent Lenahan Jr. got news that every parent dreads: Their son had been in a terrible accident.

Nineteen-year-old Kent was out with his friends, cruising Philadelphia's Main Line. He was riding on the running board of an automobile, enjoying himself and not giving any thought to how foolish and dangerous his actions were. When the car sideswiped a utility pole, the Lenahans' son was crushed between the pole and the car and then hurled to the ground. He was rushed to nearby Bryn Mawr Hospital with a fractured skull, crushed chest, and facial injuries. A broken rib had punctured one of his lungs. Kent's condition was dire, and doctors felt there was little they could do to help him. For four days his parents looked on as he languished between life and death. His temperature hit 107 degrees and his pulse was racing at 160 beats per minute—clearly his body couldn't hold out much longer. The hospital staff held no hope that he would recover.

His parents, however, were not ready to give up on their son who loved music, sports, and life. They heard reports of miraculous events attributed to a deceased Catholic priest who had served as bishop of Philadelphia from 1852 until his death in 1860. Philadelphia parishioners loved and respected Bishop John Neumann. From the time of his internment, people have visited his place of burial to pray for miracles. The account that convinced the Lenahans to join the throng of miracle seekers had taken place years earlier across the ocean. In 1923, in Italy, an eleven-year-old girl named Eva Pantani lay dying of diffused peritonitis. Last rites, a sacrament given by a priest only when death is imminent, had already been administered. Then a nun from Eva's school came to visit the critically ill girl. She brought with her a picture of Philadelphia's Bishop John Neumann. She placed the picture on the child's hopelessly diseased body and prayed, earnestly begging God for a healing touch. Miraculously, Eva was healed.

The Lenahans were desperate for a miracle, and the account of Eva's recovery gave them hope. If God would restore health to a girl in Italy through a relic of the bishop from Philadelphia, perhaps he would heal their son too. They learned that Bishop John Neumann's shrine was only ten miles away from the hospital where their son lay dying. The good bishop's body, encased in glass, was in St. Peter's Church on Fifth Street and Girard Avenue in Philadelphia. The Lenahans made their way to St. Peter's intending to acquire a relic. They obtained a piece of Bishop John Neumann's cassock, the long black garment that clergymen wear, then returned to the hospital with the scrap of fabric in hand. With prayers and great expectation, they placed the holy artifact on their son's almost lifeless body.

What was so special about Bishop Neumann that people would seek miracles through him? Why would his picture and other relics serve as the conduit for divine healing? John Neumann, an immigrant from Europe, had been Philadelphia's most beloved bishop. Born in Bohemia in 1811, he was a brilliant scholar, a hard worker, and a godly man. His heart longed to do missionary work. He came to America in 1836 to serve God, working under the authority of the Catholic Church. He organized and built churches in ethnic communities. As a gifted linguist, he was able to say Mass in the dialect of the people. Whether it was a German-speaking settlement, Irish, Italian, French, Greek, or his native Bohemian—no matter, he spoke the language fluently.

He cared deeply about education, particularly religious education. John Neumann is credited with founding the national parochial school system in the United States. Teaching was a great love of his. He loved his students and they adored him. He had a special place in his heart for minorities; as an advocate for women, blacks—both slaves and free—and poor children, he endeared himself to all but the snobbish elite. All of this made him a saint in the eyes of his parishioners and to almost everyone who knew him. Upon his untimely passing, his followers set out to have him officially declared Saint John Neumann.

However, steps to sainthood in the Catholic Church are complicated and rigorous. The very first step to becoming a bona fide saint is to have a devoted, loving following, which Neumann certainly had. This loyal dedication must prove itself by refusing to fade over the years. Devotion to Bishop John Neumann wasn't quelled with the passing of time, and this eventually led to his beatification. He was declared to be a blessed person, worthy of honor. Beatification is a precursor to being canonized, or in other words, becoming a candidate for sainthood.

What follows beatification is an investigation into the life of the candidate, not unlike the process an appointee to the U.S. Supreme Court endures. In each case, all the good one has ever accomplished is heralded, and anything less than good is dug up and exposed. These investigations are thorough and grueling. The difference is that the candidate for sainthood has already crossed over to his or her heavenly reward, probably indifferent to the judgments of man. The

Court appointee, on the other hand, is very much alive and squirming while his or her good name is alternately praised and besmirched.

There is a bit of irony in the process. A true saint is humble in nature and would probably find the attention bestowed upon him awkward and discomforting. John Neumann was just that sort of humble fellow. It probably would have killed him to be given such recognition and honor. Perhaps that's why only the deceased are beatified. However, even if a candidate's earthly life is deemed to have passed muster, there is another requirement: Proof of at least three miracles must be credited to him or her. God will work miraculously through the person who is truly a saint.

The people of John Neumann's day proclaimed that he had performed miracles. It was said that he built Catholic churches and schools with no money. That was a real tribute to his uncanny ability to administrate business and finances, but it was not the kind of miracle needed. There was no denying that Bishop Neumann's virtuous life, keen mind, and kind heart were all signs of divine influence. In 1921, the Pope declared that Neumann's life exhibited extraordinary, heroic Christian virtue. Now the Catholic Church would have to wait for God to provide three miracles as an expression of John Neumann's sainthood. They only had to wait two years for the first one—Eva Pantani's inexplicable recovery when touched by a picture of the bishop from Philadelphia was deemed John Neumann's first miracle.

Kent Lenahan's mother was hoping and praying that God would perform another miracle through a relic from the bishop. When the Lenahans returned from St. Peter's to the Bryn Mawr hospital, Kent's mother touched the piece of cloth to her son's ailing body. She prayed for a miracle, and she was not disappointed. A healing took place. Her son's pulse returned to normal, his fever broke, and he regained consciousness. There was absolutely no medical explanation for it, but he was obviously on the way to recovery.

Weeks later he walked out of the hospital and returned to his normal life. One thing was different about Kent, though. Before the accident, he wore glasses to correct his nearsighted vision. Afterward he no longer needed them. The doctors could not account for any of this other than to say, it was a miracle.

Bishop Neumann had his second miracle, and Kent Lenahan had a second chance at life. He resumed his sport of weightlifting. In a competition four years after the accident, he won both the junior and the senior division of the Middle Atlantic Amateur Athletic Union Weightlifting Championship. Musically, he continued playing trumpet, and he marched in a parade just months after leaving the hospital. Kent Lenahan went on to become a teacher and a bandleader in the Philadelphia area, thanks to a miracle.

More than ten years later, a family from New Jersey heard of the Lenahans' miracle, which inspired them to seek out a miracle for their own six-year-old son. In 1963, little Michael Flanigan was diagnosed with a rare form of bone cancer. His parents took him to John Neumann's shrine. Touching the glass coffin, they knelt and prayed for a miraculous healing for Michael. They also took a relic home with them and continued beseeching God to intervene through the bishop of Philadelphia. He did. Michael Flanigan was healed, and a third miracle was officially credited to Bishop John Neumann.

Finally, in 1977, 117 years after John Neumann died, the Catholic Church declared him Saint John Neumann. The miraculous healings of Pantani, Lenahan, and Flanigan played a huge part in the successful canonization process for Saint John. Now, three decades later, his body still lies encased in a crystal casket in the basement chapel of St. Peter the Apostle Church in Philadelphia. Believers continue to file by his shrine seeking miracles—like the one graciously bestowed upon the Kent Lenahan in 1949.

AMERICAN BANDSTAND

- 1957 -

The story of *American Bandstand* really begins in the year 1952. The world of commercial radio was being turned on its ear by a new upstart medium called television. The preceding years saw radio morph from a powerhouse entertainment machine featuring soap operas and comedies into a venue that relied heavily on musical entertainment. The largest portion of the population that was listening to radio was a new untapped market in the advertising world . . . teenagers.

In 1952 there were two major players on the teen music radio scene in Philadelphia: radio stations WPEN-AM (950) and WIP-AM (610). These stations had programs hosted by strong personalities and each played a part in the creation of *Bandstand.*

Bob Horn created a show called *Bandstand* while he was at WPEN. This pop music show and DJ Horn were extremely popular, and WIP wooed Horn to their station. One reason that Horn may have left is that WPEN had another popular music show called the *950 Club.* The *950 Club* may have presented too much competition for Horn's taste. While this show did not have the *Bandstand* name, it did have most of the other components that have come to be associated with the TV version of *Bandstand.*

The *950 Club,* hosted by Joe Grady and Ed Hurst, was also tremendously popular, especially with teens. Their show actually let teenagers into the studio to dance to their records. The show also paid homage to different high schools each day of the week.

Meanwhile another player in the game was lowly WFIL. This station was trailing the other two in the ratings race, but it did have something special that was enticing. WFIL was not only a radio station; it was also a member of the fledgling ABC television network. Bob Horn wanted to be on TV, and he allowed himself and his popular *Bandstand* program to be stolen from WIP in hopes of getting a crack at a TV spot when one became available. Horn was at first overlooked when that TV shot arose; WFIL instead offered a spot to his rivals, Grady and Hurst, with the plan to install their teen dance party on afternoon television.

One last player in this drama was hiding in the wings at WFIL. Ever since Dick Clark's days at Syracuse University, where he majored in advertising and minored in radio and worked at WEAR radio station, he had two main goals. One was to be involved in broadcasting, and the other was to make a lot of money. Clark's move to Philadelphia's WFIL was calculated from the beginning. Not only was Philadelphia one of the largest markets in the United States, Clark also saw the potential of television. He shrewdly recognized this new medium as being a very important part of the future of broadcasting. Clark's start at the bottom required him to host radio shows as a DJ but also included newscasting, and writing and reading of advertising copy. At the beginning, there was no TV for young Clark.

Dick Clark was toiling away on country music shows and all his other jobs. Clark in fact did not know much about popular music at the time—Horn, Hurst, and Grady were the real masters of that arena. When the TV option became available, Hurst and Grady could not break their contract with WPEN, so Horn got his big TV break after all.

In the early 1950s WFIL had a terrible track record with its daytime TV schedule. The ABC network provided evening programming but had no national daytime programming at all. The second-rate Hollywood movies that were played in the afternoons drew minimal viewers and ABC was being trounced in the ratings by NBC and CBS, both of whom were providing daytime programming for all their affiliates.

Bob Horn's first whack at television was a poorly conceived show mixing old music clips with live interviews of just about anyone Horn could talk onto the show. While this offering fared poorly, Horn was not going down without a fight. He fought to bring his radio *Bandstand* program to TV using the *950 Club* format with a live dancing audience.

WFIL executives felt the show would need co-hosts (like the *950 Club*'s duo of Hurst and Grady) and brought Lee Stewart into the mix. Lee Stewart was simply a mistake. The forced pairing of Stewart and Horn did not make any sense. Stewart's background did not prepare him for this type of show and there was no real chemistry between the two men. This did not sit well with Horn, but he was powerless to stop the decision of the management. WFIL proceeded to remake the studio into a mock record store and decorate the walls with pennants representing all the local high schools.

Bandstand made its television debut on October 6, 1952. WFIL's biggest fear was that they might televise an empty studio. In an effort to ensure a studio audience, WFIL put together a tremendous promotional campaign targeting high school students. The campaign was successful! Some 1,500 kids showed up that first Tuesday. The panicked producer, Tony Mammarella, quickly organized the teens into groups that were rotated in and out of the studio every half hour. WFIL had the makings of an instant success. The music played, the kids danced, and most importantly, people watched. The show aired daily from 3:30 to 4:45 p.m.

Bob Horn introduced a few new twists to the original *950 Club* format. One of the most enduring additions was the Rate-A-Record segment. Pre-selected teens were given an opportunity to give a numerical rating to one of the hot new records being played. This gave birth to the phrase that would forever be associated with *American Bandstand:* "I'll give it a 92 because it's got a great beat and it's easy to dance to." Horn also came up with the idea of having current recording artists appear live in the studio for an interview, a chance to plug their record, and to lip-sync their record on TV. He would welcome these performers to the show with a booming, "We've got company!"

All these factors combined to create a runaway hit in Philadelphia. Of course there were problems. Bob Horn and Lee Stewart were at odds from the beginning. Added to that strain was the fact that both Horn and Stewart were middle-aged men, and neither made a very good appearance on TV with the teenage viewers. While Horn was ultimately successful at getting Stewart yanked from the show, he would face a more disturbing fate.

Bob Horn reveled in his celebrity and power. He was flamboyant and very much in the public view. Slowly his personal life began to unravel as well. Bob Horn, married with three young daughters, became implicated in an affair with at least one of the teenage girls from his audience. As this information was coming to light, Horn was also involved in a drunk driving incident. One of the pet projects of media magnate Walter Annenberg, who owned WFIL, was a crackdown on drunk driving, and WFIL dumped Horn because of the drunk driving incident to avoid the completely devastating details that would be coming from the police vice department.

The very clear choice to succeed Bob Horn was Dick Clark. He was young, clean-cut, ambitious, and without blemishes. He had been in the wings during everything that occurred—while Horn was living the high life, the unassuming Clark had been promoted to host of the radio version of Horn's old-style *Bandstand*, and Clark even got to stand in for Horn on TV when Horn took vacation time. Clark knew what to do and how to do it. WFIL needed this squeaky-clean guy to offset any damage done to the station and its cash-cow hit TV show.

Clark moved smoothly into the hosting job. His business acumen came to the forefront almost immediately as he began to build his music empire. Little by little he insinuated himself into the unseen workings of the record industry. Clark invested in record companies, artist management firms, and even a company that manufactured records, allowing him to capitalize on his own success. It was not uncommon for the artists appearing on his TV show to be at least partially managed by one of his companies. Furthermore, the records being promoted were from companies he owned or had an interest in. Even companies that had no direct connection to Dick Clark were including Clark in schemes that netted the young host a profit. Records played on *Bandstand* sold like hotcakes all through the Philadelphia area.

There was only one cloud on Clark's *Bandstand* horizon. The ABC television network was straining to catch up with its bigger competitors. ABC desperately needed to compete with NBC and CBS and was actively seeking daytime programming of its own. But if ABC began broadcasting daytime programming, Dick Clark would be out of a very lucrative job.

Dick Clark became a man with a mission. If ABC was going start afternoon programming, Clark wanted *Bandstand* to be a part of it.

He made sure that the executives at ABC got kinescopes of the show. He made phone calls. He even drove to New York City on repeated occasions to hawk his product directly to those in charge.

To the network's credit, they did recognize the success *Bandstand* enjoyed in the Philadelphia market—the show, after all, was a juggernaut. However, they doubted its ability to appeal to a national audience, and there was also the issue of race—*Bandstand* had always been integrated.

In the 1950s the country was gearing up for the civil rights movement. The early signs of change were present everywhere, but *Bandstand* was not a perfect model for integration. African Americans were underrepresented in the studio audience, and while this portion of the population was not discouraged from attending the show, they certainly weren't encouraged either. But many African-American artists appeared on the show, and there were certainly African-American teens dancing in the studio. This was pretty heady stuff in the '50s. But an even bigger sticking point was that rock 'n' roll has its roots in African-American rhythm and blues. Not only were white artists recording a type of music that had traditionally been associated with black artists, they were re-recording songs originally sung by black artists to make them more palatable to the music-buying white teenagers. This certainly caused some ruffled feathers.

ABC executives had to question how an integrated show would "sell" in other parts of the country—especially the South. Fortunately for Dick Clark and company, the network's search for appropriate programming was proving difficult at best. WFIL came to the rescue by making an impressive offer: They would provide ABC with *Bandstand* for free.

At this time ABC had sixty-seven affiliates around the country, but that only represented about 12 percent of the nation's TV stations. NBC and CBS were already broadcasting in color and ABC was still strictly black-and-white. In other words, ABC was not just trailing; they were a distant third. Money was a huge issue. WFIL's generous offer could not be ignored.

ABC's assistant director of programming, Ted Fetter, is officially considered the man responsible for lining up *Bandstand*. Fetter said years later in an interview that he did not pick Dick Clark . . . Dick Clark picked him.

Aside from the name change, very few alterations were needed to dress up *Bandstand* for a national audience. The studio at WFIL got a minor facelift. Gone were the local high school pennants, but the fake-record-store theme still ruled. Tony Mammarella was still the producer, Dick Clark was still the host, and the cast of regular high school dancers still rated the records. The regulars had already become celebrities in their own community; now they were about to be introduced to the entire country.

On August 5, 1957, good old Philadelphia *Bandstand* was transformed into *American Bandstand*. Special guests Billy Williams and the Chordettes spoke with Dick Clark about their newest recordings. Clark spun the wax while the Philly faithful danced.

Most of the critics were not exactly blown away. *Billboard* wrote, "As a sociological study of teenage behavior, the premiere was a mild success." But critics are usually very good at criticizing and often very unreliable at predicting hits.

ABC had only agreed to a two-week trial of this quirky new show. By the end of the first week, the A. C. Nielsen Company reported that *American Bandstand* had pulled in about twenty million viewers. These were astounding numbers! ABC gained at least three new affiliates that week. During the second week more than ten new affiliated stations joined the ABC family. A third week was added to the trial. ABC started signing new stations at a rate of three per week. *American Bandstand* was a runaway hit with the whole country—this one small program effectively built ABC into a competitive third network.

A bonus for the network was *who* was watching the show. Yes, millions of teenagers across the country were watching, but so were young housewives. It was an advertiser's dream come true. The burgeoning population of young families had money to spend and the network could take advantage of the multitude of stay-at-home moms.

ABC teamed with Dick Clark on other projects and there were many more successes for nearly everyone involved. But the story of *American Bandstand* continued for decades. It was one of the most successful shows ever broadcast in the history of television. *American Bandstand* helped spawn the enormous record industry and made stars out of countless artists. Finally, like its millions of teen viewers, *American Bandstand* ushered a major television network from its juvenile days to adulthood.

WILT'S 100

- 1962 -

IT IS AN AMAZING RECORD IN THE ANNALS of the National Basketball Association: In one game, Wilton Norman Chamberlain scored one hundred points for the Philadelphia Warriors against the New York Knicks. Many believe that this record will stand forever. Forever is a long time, but as of this writing the record has stood for an astounding forty-five years. And that record was set on a cold slushy day at a home game for the Philadelphia Warriors in . . . Hershey, Pennsylvania?

Yes, the Philadelphia Warriors had their off-season training camp in Hershey and played a couple of home games in that arena as a tribute to their out-of-town fans. So even though the game didn't take place in downtown Philadelphia, it was a Philadelphia "home game."

Wilt Chamberlain was already a sensation in the NBA. At seven feet, one inch, he was the biggest of the big men in basketball. He was also considered one of the strongest, if not *the* strongest player in the game. And when it came to talent, many believe Wilt had gone through the line twice. All of this had been obvious to basketball fans back when Wilt was in college in Kansas. But Philadelphia basketball fans knew all about him long before his college years.

Wilt Chamberlain was a homegrown product. At six feet, ten inches and still growing, he was the most amazing high school basketball player that anyone had ever seen. He also excelled in other sports, which highlighted his natural athletic ability.

Although Wilt was a smash success in college, he decided to leave school to pursue a professional career. The rules of the day did not allow him to play in the National Basketball Association, so Wilt spent one year as a member of the world-famous Harlem Globetrotters. In his memoirs he claimed that to be the happiest time of his professional career.

The Philadelphia Warriors used the fact that Wilt was from Philadelphia to claim him for their team when he left college. So after his stint with the Globetrotters, Wilt "the stilt" suited up with the Warriors.

His high-scoring game was not televised, so there is no lasting video record of the event. According to his Warrior teammates, Wilt was destined to have a monster day on the basketball court that day. He had already beaten his teammates at cards and won every game of chance and skill at a local arcade.

Another factor that contributed to the big day was the absence of Phil Jordan, starting center for the New York Knicks. At six feet, ten inches, Jordan was one of the few NBA players who provided Wilt with serious competition, but he watched this game from the sidelines due to an injury. That left backup center Daryl Imhoff with the impossible task of guarding the leading scorer in the league.

Wilt Chamberlain accumulated twenty-three points in the first quarter. For any other player in the NBA that would be considered a fantastic total for an entire game. By half time the tall man's point total was forty-one. Wilt's teammates realized the potential by this point and started feeding him the ball. During the third quarter Wilt made twenty points from the floor and an additional eight points from the free-throw line, which shows it really was a special day—the truth is that Wilt Chamberlain was lousy from the free-throw line. His point total at the start of the fourth quarter was sixty-nine.

The "Big Dipper," as he was affectionately called, sank three straight baskets to start the last quarter of the game. At this point the crowd of only 4,124 fans began to chant, "Give it to Wilt!" The fans that braved the cold weather were not disappointed. Points ninety-nine and one hundred came on one of Chamberlain's trademark dunks with forty-six seconds remaining on the clock. Pandemonium broke out in the arena. Wilt Chamberlain had just set a new NBA record for the most points in one game surpassing the record of 78 points which was held by . . . Wilt Chamberlain!

The final score was Philadelphia 169, New York 147. Daryl Imhoff watched the end of the game from the sidelines—he and four of his New York teammates fouled out of the game in their attempt to contain Wilt Chamberlain.

The hundred-point game was just one of the many highlights for Wilt in the 1961–1962 season. He averaged a record 50.4 points a game that season, averaged 25.7 rebounds per game, and scored a mind-boggling 4,029 points for the season. He is the only player in history to top four thousand points. In fact, only one other player has scored more than three thousand points—Michael Jordan in the 1986–1987 season. Jordan's 3,041-point total trails Wilt by nearly one thousand!

THE SNOWBALL SANTA INCIDENT

- 1968 -

IT WAS A COLD, SNOWY DECEMBER DAY AT old Franklin Field in Philadelphia. The hometown Eagles were hosting the Minnesota Vikings in a professional football game. There was a capacity crowd of more than fifty thousand fans packed into the stadium. One reason for the large crowd was the planned half-time celebration that included a gala Christmas pageant. The more important reason for the full house is that Philadelphia fans are real fans—among the most knowledgeable and energetic fans in the country. Conversely those same fans have a reputation for being pretty tough. In December of 1968 the fans had a lot to be disgruntled about.

The year 1968 was not a good year for the Philadelphia Eagles football franchise. Coming into the final game of the year with the Vikings, the team had only managed two wins all year and had already accumulated eleven losses.

Many other factors caused well-informed fans to boil with emotion on the inside. Some believed that Eagles owner Jerry Wolman was systematically dismantling their team. Mr. Wolman had hired Joe Kuharich as not only the head coach, but also the general manager for the team. At the all-important quarterback position, Kuharich traded perennial all-pro and Hall of Famer Sonny Jurgenson to the division rival Washington Redskins. In return the Eagles got journeyman Norm Snead. While Norm was considered competent he paled in comparison to Sonny's bright star. This trade did not sit well with the Philly fan base and certainly caused a number of boos from the stands. It was also the foundation of a saying that lingers to this day around the city: "Joe must go!"

This combination of factors produced a rather sour mood among Eagles fans on December 15 as their team struggled through the first half of the game. The fans were cold, wet, and unhappy, and they were letting their team know how they felt. The bright spot of the day was about to unfold as the crowd looked forward to the half-time Christmas celebration. They were in for yet another big disappointment.

The weather was not exactly cooperating; in fact the weather was terrible. Snow and sleet had caused problems all over town and the football field was a mess. Some members of the pageant, including Santa Claus, never made it to the field that day. The conditions had turned the playing field into a muddy mess, and the staff at Franklin Field determined that driving the floats out onto the field would cause even more trouble, so they decided to cancel the floats. A last-ditch effort was put together hastily and an enterprising staff member spotted a fan in the crowd dressed as Santa Claus.

When watching a football game outdoors in the winter, some fans might have a nip or two from a bottle to ward off the cold; this may very well have been the case with the emergency replacement Kris Kringle, Frank Olivo.

Frank was nineteen years old at the time, and he was and is a diehard Philadelphia Eagles fan. He was not much of a Santa Claus, though. In fact he was a skinny kid in an ill-fitting Santa suit with a very obviously fake white beard. But Frank was game and took to his new duties with gusto and good humor. His mission was to parade across the field in the company of the illustrious Philadelphia Eagles cheerleaders. What nineteen-year-old fan is going to say no to that job?

Many fans found this spectacle hilarious; some saw it as ridiculous. Others, who may have been letting out their disappointment with the team, the weather, and the lack of a real show, reacted with less than good humor. That's right, they booed Santa Claus.

Amid screams of "Joe must go!" and a variety of jeers and boos, the hometown crowd started to get into the act, finding that the weather had provided the perfect ammunition for just such a situation: snowballs! As Frank/Santa reached the end zone, the snow began to fly.

A local news reporter named Ray Didinger claimed that Mr. Olivo was visibly intoxicated and believes that may have egged the crowd on. Taunts about Frank's suitability as Santa Claus mingled with the jeering of Joe Kuharich, Jerry Wolman, and the entire Philadelphia Eagles organization.

According to one account, Frank laughed off the non-lethal snowball attack as he jokingly pointed out the rabblerousers, then warned that there were going to be some empty stockings this Christmas. The reaction from the crowd was swift and predictable—a lot more snowballs.

Monday Night Football commentator Howard Cosell took the opportunity to denounce Eagles fans in no uncertain terms and the story of the fans that snowballed Santa was born.

For Frank Olivo, the incident was no big deal. He was a fan himself, after all, and who would better understand the fan frustration that day? Yet when asked if he might consider playing Santa Claus next year, his response was quick: "No way. If it doesn't snow, they'll probably throw beer bottles."

Fans of Philadelphia do have a well-deserved reputation for being rough and fanatical. In 1997 law enforcement has actually set up camp in the Eagles football stadium, and it became the first stadium to contain a courtroom and jail for the more serious offenders. While some point to this as proof that Philadelphia fans are incorrigible, others see it as a positive step toward making the whole experience better for fans everywhere.

Snowballs and Philadelphia football fans have one more story of note. On December 10, 1989, a game with the hated Dallas Cowboys came to be known as the "Bounty Bowl II." Once more there was a snowstorm, and again the staff at the stadium was unable to remove all the snow by game time. Once again the snowballs flew freely. Most were aimed at the Cowboys coaching staff and players. One fan in particular admitted later to getting caught up in the moment and wagering twenty dollars with a friend that he couldn't reach the field with a snowball. The confessing culprit admitted to losing the bet, but went on to gain fame in his own right: He became mayor of Philadelphia and later was elected governor of Pennsylvania; his name is Ed Rendell.

On the day they snowballed Santa, the Philadelphia Eagles lost against the Minnesota Vikings to end their season with a dismal 2 and 12 record. Perhaps the moral of the story is, if you want to win the game, don't mess with Santa!

AN ELUSIVE KILLER

- 1976 -

Soldiers are trained to be alert and on the lookout for enemies. In times of war, they remain on guard against assault and ambush. Watchfulness often saves lives; but vigilance is of little use if the enemy is unknown and invisible. When the American Legionnaires of Pennsylvania came to Philadelphia in 1976, they had no reason to watch out for enemies. They came for a celebration—their annual state convention.

In the bicentennial year of our nation, Philadelphia was the ideal location for the American Legion State Convention. From July 21 through 24, both young and old veterans gathered at the illustrious Bellevue-Stratford Hotel. Built at the turn of the century, the hotel was a massive structure with plenty of room for conventioneers to congregate. Although it was an old building, modern conveniences had been added throughout the years—most notably, an air-conditioning system. The weather in July is typically hot, and during the third week of July 1976, a heat wave broiled the East Coast. Air-conditioning at the Bellevue-Stratford ran non-stop.

A group of three legionnaires from a small town north of Harrisburg made the trek to Philadelphia in high spirits, eager to participate in the convention and enjoy a mid-summer getaway. One of them, James Dolan, hadn't been feeling well. He considered bowing out of the trip, but he didn't want to let his buddies down, so he decided to go along. Perhaps the time away would do him some good. He packed up and took off with the other two guys. They traveled together, roomed together, and spent most of their time in Philly together. Even though Jim was a bit under the weather, they all had a good time.

The four-day convention was packed with activities: business sessions, ceremonies, and times of revelry. Moments were set aside to solemnly remember fallen comrades and to reminisce. Veterans enjoyed reunions, both organized and spontaneous. Food and drink were plentiful, and there was no lack of late-night partying. So it was no wonder that some legionnaires were feeling poorly after the convention. Their friends joked about the rotten effects of too much alcohol, assuming their comrades were suffering from hangovers. But soon, word was out that the afflicted legionnaires were critically ill. Then came reports of the first death. All joking ceased; frivolity was replaced with shock, disbelief . . . and fear.

When Jim Dolan returned home, he was so sick he had to be hospitalized. Only a few days later, one of his travel companions was also admitted to the hospital. Their symptoms were the same: raging fever, headache, muscle aches, and congestion. It was as if they had pneumonia, but this pneumonia wouldn't respond to customary treatment. Doctors were at a loss, baffled because these patients were only in their late thirties and early forties. They were too young to die. They ought to be able to fight off pneumonia—if that's what had attacked them. But whatever it was couldn't be defeated. Jim Dolan died first, then his good friend and fellow veteran succumbed as well.

The third man in their party, Jim's cousin, also became ill, but not critically so. Another legionnaire had bunked in with them for two nights of the convention, yet miraculously he escaped any sign of illness.

That was part of the mystery. Two or more legionnaires, who shared the same room, ate the same food, and participated in the same activities, met different fates. Many came through unscathed, others got terribly sick, and some died. A number of the victims were overnight guests in the Bellevue-Stratford, but not all. Husbands and wives attended together; one in a couple might get sick, the other would remain healthy. The disease was like a sniper randomly choosing his prey.

Finding a cause for what was now being called Legionnaires' disease was paramount to finding a cure. Investigators from the Centers for Disease Control (CDC) were called upon to make some sense of this inexplicable ailment. Medical detectives searched out every imaginable contributing factor, from water to food to the possibility of sabotage. CDC officials worked diligently to determine if this was a viral illness or an infectious disease. Their job was to figure out what toxins, fungi, or bacteria were involved and how the illness was spread. The investigation was already difficult enough but faced a further complication: Concurrent to the outbreak of Legionnaires' disease was public panic over a strain of influenza called swine flu. There was a perceived threat of an epidemic outbreak of this deadly flu. Government officials were debating the necessity of nationwide vaccinations, but if this illness attacking legionnaires turned out to be the highly contagious swine flu, it would already be too late. The result could be devastating.

On August 4, the *Philadelphia Inquirer* alerted the public: "Mystery Death Toll Reaches 20." Another day, a sad story had the headline, "Legionnaires bury one member, pray for the next one who dies." It was becoming evident that only those who had been to

Philadelphia were among the sick and dying. Relatives were not infected when their legionnaire returned home from the convention. Apparently the disease wasn't contagious; swine flu could be ruled out. Medical scientists had previously eliminated the possibility that bacteria caused the illness. By the eighth of August the newspaper reported that there were twenty-five deaths and still no answers. Suspicion held that the American Legionnaires had been poisoned, either intentionally or inadvertently. Medical detectives shifted their focus to toxins. Allegations of deliberate poisoning led to a thorough inspection of the building that functioned as headquarters during the convention, the Bellevue-Stratford. But no indication of foul play was found, putting to rest notions of sabotage. Further scrutiny of the hotel was in order.

As part of the probe, samples were taken from everywhere in the old hotel. Air, water, and dust were collected for testing. Residue and grime were even scraped out of air ducts and water pipes. Although nothing definitive turned up, the hotel had to be temporarily closed. Something had sickened 155 people and killed twenty-nine others, and the only common denominator was the Bellevue-Stratford Hotel. An ailing Legion Auxiliary member went to the hospital with fever, chills, and headache. When doctors heard she had helped serve food at the Bellevue during the convention, she was immediately treated for Legionnaires' disease. The name of the building alone had become a red flag, and that bad press dealt a deathblow to the grand old hotel.

Closing the doors put five hundred people out of work. All of those people were another part of the mystery—if the illness had been contracted in the hotel, why weren't employees affected? Also, there was a huge Eucharist Conference at the Bellevue the week after the American Legion Convention. Of more than 350 people who stayed there, and hundreds more who walked in to attend meetings, only two Catholic delegates became ill with pneumonia. Doctors confirmed symptoms of Legionnaires' disease in each of them, but neither became critically ill. CDC investigators were stumped. By the end of August no new cases were showing up, the wounded were healing, and the casualties were buried. For lack of new evidence, the search was winding down. Within months, the investigation was all but closed. It seemed that Legionnaires' disease would forever remain an unsolved mystery.

Five months after the outbreak—in December of 1976—Dr. Joseph McDade tried one more time to solve the case. Thanks to his tenacity, Dr. McDade, a CDC laboratory scientist, successfully identified the culprit responsible for Legionnaires' disease—legionella pneumophila. This bacterium was found to grow in contaminated water systems, defective cooling towers, and in some cases, showerheads. Even condensation exposed to intense heat over time can breed this lethal microbe. Rather disconcerting was the news that it had been causing deaths for centuries but had never been pinned down because of its elusive nature; it no sooner strikes than it vanishes. In most cases, by the time the evil bacteria sickens people, the source has gone away without a trace.

The enemy that attacked American Legionnaires was bacteria after all. It began growing when the heat wave of late July put a strain on the hotel's outdated air-conditioning system. Either the overworked cooling equipment, or its proximity to the hotel's incinerator, provided an environment for the bacteria to grow. The old ductwork in the building dispersed the deadly microbes throughout the hotel, and unsuspecting people breathed in the contaminated air. Fortunately, not everyone who inhaled the contaminated air was susceptible to the disease. Healthy individuals, exposed continually to the toxic microbes—hotel employees, for example—built up antibodies that protected them from getting sick.

Legionnaires were the victims of this obscure and mysterious enemy, but it could have been anyone who was unlucky enough to have a compromised health condition and be in the wrong place at the wrong time. From this sad episode medical scientists traced and named the elusive killer. Although it hasn't been eradicated, antibiotics have been developed to combat it. There are deaths attributed to Legionnaires' disease every year. This enemy still makes sneak attacks, but it is no longer unknown nor undetectable. Knowing what they are up against gives people a fighting chance.

MILLION-DOLLAR MANIA

- 1981 -

JOEY COYLE WAS JUST ANOTHER KID from the neighborhood in South
Philly. He was well liked and friendly, but he was also an under-
achiever. At the age of twenty-nine he lived at home with his ailing
mother. He worked off and on at the docks as a longshoreman and
he was hooked on methamphetamine.

On one particular day in 1981 Joey was looking for drugs, but
he had a dilemma—he had no money. His mother's condition had
deteriorated and she had recently moved out of her own home to stay
with Joey's sister. Joey's father had passed away years before. Joey was
waiting for a check from his last stint on the docks, but he felt con-
fident that he could con his dealer into fronting him some drugs.

With this thought in mind Joey strolled over to his neighbor's
house. Twenty-one-year-old John Behlau was busy doing bodywork
on his father's 1971 maroon Chevy Malibu. John had just finished
putting some blue primer paint on the right front fender of the well-
used car. John's friend Jed Pennock—at age twenty, the baby of the

group—was sitting around and literally watching the paint dry. These three young men were about to embark on an amazing journey.

They piled into the Chevy and set off to see Joey's drug connection. That endeavor proved to be fruitless. The drug dealer wasn't home, so the boys headed back to the neighborhood using back roads that were in disrepair. As the car bumped its way down Swanson Street, Joey called out to John to stop. He had spotted a yellow box with wheels lying in the roadway and thought the scavenged item might make a nice toolbox.

As the car shuddered to a stop beside the box, Joey leaned out his door and jerked the box upright. He was rewarded with the surprise of his life. As Joey wrestled with the box, its contents spilled out into the street. Two large canvas bags with some kind of lead seal caught Joey's full attention. He dragged one into the car and noticed the lettering on the bag. It said "Federal Reserve Bank." Joey scampered out of the car, grabbed the other bag, jumped back in, and shouted, "Move it! Let's roll!"

As John steered toward their street, Joey found a pen and used it to rip into the first bag. That's when things got real interesting.

The bag seemed to contain nothing but bundles of hundred-dollar bills. The three young men whooped and shouted and laughed—they didn't know it yet, but they had just found $1.2 million in unmarked cold, hard cash.

One might wonder exactly how $1.2 million ended up sitting in the middle of a barely used back street in South Philadelphia. It may be hard to believe, but it literally fell off the back of a truck.

The truck in question was owned and operated by the Purolator Armored Car Company and manned by two of their personnel, Bill Proctor and Ralph Saracino, who would soon be making their way to the unemployment line. When a person misplaces $1.2 million at work, he doesn't expect a promotion.

Bill and Ralph had discovered that the money was missing just moments after they lost it. They were right around the corner, just past the second gate of Purolator's building, when another employee pointed out their open back door. Bill and Ralph rushed to retrace their steps. Amazingly, the money had only been missing for about three minutes. Yet when the pair arrived back at the scene all they found was an empty yellow box. In just a few minutes, a number of lives were changed forever.

The police were notified immediately and the case was handled by one of Philadelphia's finest, named Pat Laurenzi. All suspicions were placed squarely on the heads of Bill Proctor and Ralph Saracino. But of course they didn't steal anything.

Over at the crime scene the police found a witness. Thomas Piacentino saw the whole thing, and he had an eye for detail. He described the box falling off the truck, the few cars that swerved to avoid the box, and the maroon Chevy Malibu with the blue painted fender that stopped. Thomas described the young, sandy-haired man that grabbed the white bags and threw them in the Malibu. Thomas then told how he and his brother Charles walked over to look at the yellow box just as the Purolator truck came flying back.

Meanwhile back at the Coyle house the boys had gathered in Joey's bedroom. They were dancing, laughing, jumping, and slapping each other. This was just too good to be true. Slowly, but surely, reality started to set in. Whose money was this? Who would be looking for it? Joey considered the cash to be his. He found it and it was an unquestionable case of finders keepers. After all, he had done nothing illegal . . . or so he believed.

The reality was that this was illegal. The law clearly states that anything found with a value in excess of $250 must be turned over to the authorities. Joey was not aware of this fine point of law. His first action was to tell the boys to keep the whole escapade under their hats. "Don't tell anyone" was his new mantra. But privately his friends were thinking about the possible reward money.

While Joey's plan to keep the story quiet was good in principle, it was more difficult in the real world. Joey went back out to score drugs and then proceeded to tell half the neighborhood about his good fortune. Over the next day or two he enlisted various friends, acquaintances, and even some mob guys to help him attempt to launder—and more importantly keep—the money.

Each day the pressure increased. The money kept getting split into smaller portions with different characters dipping into the well. Joey was partying a lot, enjoying his drug of choice as well as finding comfort in alcohol. The number of people that knew the truth just kept spreading all over South Philly.

Detective Pat Laurenzi was methodically plodding along Joey's trail. From the beginning he knew he was looking for a maroon Chevy Malibu with one blue fender. When a car fitting that description showed up in a parking lot in New Jersey, Laurenzi quickly traced it back to John Behlau's dad. One by one the pieces to the puzzle fell into place. As the detective gathered information and evidence, it became clear that the money was spread around the neighborhood. Some of the parties involved volunteered money back. Others bartered for reward money. One even hired a lawyer to negotiate the best deal.

Eventually, everybody fingered Joey, but Joey was playing his own game of finders keepers. He managed to elude the law and stay high on drugs and alcohol. But his pot of gold was dwindling—he was down to about two hundred thousand dollars in about five days. He knew he needed a new plan, and he decided to leave the country.

On the sixth day after Joey found the money, he talked a friend into driving him to New York City. Frank Santos had connections—his ex-wife was in the travel business. It was decided that Joey would fly to Mexico because you didn't need a passport to enter the country and the United States had no extradition deal with Mexico. Frank's ex bought the ticket in Frank's name and the two set off for the Big Apple.

After a harrowing night in New York City and the loss of even more of the money, the pair headed to Kennedy airport. Joey was busy in the men's room trying to hide on his body the more than one hundred thousand dollars remaining. When he finally tried to board his plane, he was accosted by the police (dying his hair black had fooled no one) and Joey and Frank were headed back to Philadelphia with a police escort to face the music. The entire adventure had lasted just one week.

Back in Philadelphia, Joey became a folk hero. Newspaper articles and stories on TV depicted him as a modern-day Robin Hood. Many of his contemporaries felt that they might do the same thing in his position. After all, the money fell off a truck. It's not like he stole it.

The prosecuting attorney had a different view. Joey was formally charged. One of the biggest problems he faced was the fact that $196,400 was never recovered. To Assistant District Attorney Robert Casey that made Joey Coyle a thief.

As the trial played out, it became clear that many of Joey's fellow Philadelphians considered his actions to be less than a real crime. In the end Joey Coyle won his court battle—the jury let him go.

As time passed a movie called *Money for Nothing* starring John Cusack was made based on Joey's story. A number of details were either glossed over or just plain changed, and the movie was not a box office success. One reason the movie might have suffered is the sad fate of Joey Coyle: Three weeks before the movie opened, Joey Coyle committed suicide.

Money didn't solve Joey Coyle's problems in life; it only made them worse. Still, it's hard to predict what anyone might do if a million dollars fell into his lap.

FAMOUS PHILADELPHIANS

The list of famous people from Philadelphia is so long, it could not possibly be reproduced here. The following are some of the highlights.

Louisa May Alcott, writer
Marian Anderson, singer
Frankie Avalon, singer
Kevin Bacon, actor
Chuck Barris, game show host
Sydney Biddle Barrows, madam
Ethel Barrymore, actress
John Barrymore, actor
Lionel Barrymore, actor
Jerry Blavat, radio personality
Guion Bluford, astronaut
Danny Bonaduce, actor
Peter Boyle, actor
Ed Bradley, newsman
David Brenner, comedian
Kobe Bryant, athlete
Roy Campanella, athlete
Wilt Chamberlain, athlete
Chubby Checker, singer
Noam Chomsky, linguist
Randall "Tex" Cobb, boxer
Imogene Coca, actress

John Coltrane, musician
Bill Cosby, comedian/actor
Broderick Crawford, actor
Jim Croce, singer/songwriter
R. Crumb, cartoonist
Blythe Danner, actress
James Darren, actor
Kim Delaney, actress
Curly Joe Dorita, comic/actor
Mike Douglas, talk show host
Ja'net Du Bois, actress
Angelo Dundee, boxing manager
Kevin Eubanks, musician
Fabian, singer
Lola Falana, actress
Norman Fell, actor
Tina Fey, writer/actress
W. C. Fields, comedian
Larry Fine, comic/actor
Eddie Fisher, singer
Joe Frazier, boxer
Richard Gere, actor
Seth Green, actor
Benjamin Guggenheim, philanthropist
Alexander Haig, politician
Daryl Hall, singer
Alexander Hamilton, politician
Sherman Hemsley, actor
Billie Holiday, singer
Kevin Hooks, actor
Joan Jett, singer

Grace Kelly, actress/princess

Walt Kelly, cartoonist

Jack Klugman, actor

Patti LaBelle, singer

Mario Lanza, singer

Joey Lawrence, actor

David Lynch, director

Al Martino, singer

George McClellan, civil war general

Jim McKay, sports announcer

Margaret Mead, anthropologist

Harold Melvin, singer

Dennis Miller, comedian

Zero Mostel, actor

The Nicholas Brothers, dancers

John Oates, singer

John Joseph O'Connor, Cardinal

William Paley, television executive

Holly Robinson Peete, actress

Teddy Pendergrass, singer

Ed Rendell, politician

David Rittenhouse, scientist

Paul Robeson, actor

Betsy Ross, seamstress

Todd Rundgren, singer/producer

Benjamin Rush, physician

Bobby Rydell, singer

Bob Saget, comedian/actor

Dee Dee Sharp, singer

M. Night Shyamalan, director

Penny Singleton, actress

Will Smith, actor/rapper
Arlen Specter, politician
Parker Stevenson, actor
Teller (of Penn and Teller), magician
Nancy Walker, actress
John Wanamaker, merchant
Ethel Waters, singer
Andrew Wyeth, painter

BIBLIOGRAPHY

Go Fly a Kite—1752

Brands, H. W. *The First American: The Life and Times of Benjamin Franklin.* New York: Doubleday, 2000.

Cohen, I. Bernard. *Benjamin Franklin's Science.* Cambridge, MA, and London, England: Harvard University Press, 1990.

"The Electric Ben Franklin." www.ushistory.org/franklin/info/kite.htm.

Isaacson, Walter. *Benjamin Franklin: An American Life.* New York: Simon & Schuster, 2003.

The Transit of Venus—1769

Godcharles, Frederic A. *Daily Stories of Pennsylvania.* Chicago: W. B. Conkey Company, 1924.

Mitton, Jacqueline. *Cambridge Dictionary of Astronomy.* New York: Cambridge University Press, 2001.

Moore, Patrick. *Venus.* London: Cassell Illustrated, 2002.

Moore, Patrick, ed. *The Astronomy Encyclopedia.* New York: Oxford University Press, 2002.

A Housewife Spy Completes Her Mission—1777

Bohrer, Melissa Lukeman. *Glory, Passion, and Principle: The Story of Eight Remarkable Women at the Core of the American Revolution.* New York: Atria Books, 2003.

Boudinot, Colonel Elias. *Memoirs.* Personal journal, 1906.

"Lydia Darragh." www.ushistory.org/march/bio/lydia.htm.

Meschianza—1778

Baskin, Marg. "The Mischianza." *Banecdotes.* http://home.golden .net/~marg/bansite/banecdotes/80mischianza.html.

Crary, Catherine S. *The Price of Loyalty: Tory Writings from the Revolutionary Era.* New York: McGraw Hill, 1973.

Godcharles, Frederic A. *Daily Stories of Pennsylvania.* Chicago: W. B. Conkey Company, 1924.

Inverse Theater. "A Word to the Wise: Meschianza." *News from the Inverse Theater,* June 2002. www.inversetheater.org/Newsletter/ v020601.htm

Jackson, John W. *With the British Army in Philadelphia 1777–1778.* San Rafael, CA: Presidio Press, 1979.

National Jousting Association. "The Tournaments of Colonial Times." www.nationaljousting.com/history/colonial.htm.

The Doans Are Done—1787

"Buckingham Township, Bucks County, Pennsylvania." http://en
.wikipedia.org/wiki/Buckingham_Township%2C_Bucks_
County%2C_Pennsylvania.

Doane College. "Doane Family Association of America, Inc., 47th
Biennial Reunion." www.doane.edu/About_Doane/Info/
Doane_Family/Reunions/Archives/.

Godcharles, Frederic A. *Daily Stories of Pennsylvania*. Chicago:
W. B. Conkey Company, 1924.

Mulcahy, Peter. "The Doans in Bucks County: The Life and Times
of the Plumstead Cowboys." www.peterprints.com/doanes.htm.

Piper Tavern. "History Since 1778." www.pipertavern.com/artpages/
history.htm.

Record of the Volunteers of the United States. July 1839.

First in Liberty; First in Robbery—1798

"Bank Robbery." http://en.wikipedia.org/wiki/Bank_robbery.

"Carpenters' Hall." www.carpentershall.org/.

"The Great Bank Heist of 1798." http://ushistory.org/carpenter
shall/visit/bank.htm.

Lyon, Patrick. *Narrative of Patrick Lyon Who Suffered Three Months
Severe Imprisonment in Philadelphia Gaol on Merely a Vague Suspi-
cion of Being Concerned in a Robbery of the Bank of Pennsylvania
With his Remarks Thereon.* Philadelphia: Carpenters' Hall, 1799.

Swierczynski, Duane. *This Here's a Stick-Up: The Big Bad Book of American Bank Robbery.* New York: Alpha, 2002.

The Riots of 1844—1844

Feldberg, Michael. *The Philadelphia Riots of 1844: A Study of Ethnic Conflict.* Westport, CT: Greenwood Press, 1975.

Fitzgerald, Margaret E. "The Philadelphia Nativist Riots." *The Hedgemaster,* 2002. www.irish-society.org/Hedgemaster %20Archives/philadelphia.htm.

Historical Society of Pennsylvania. www.hsp.org/default .aspx?id=394.

The Sad Fate of the Swimming Elephants—1847

Daily Mercury, April 1874.

Frei, Georges. "Swimming Elephants." Translated by Penny Adams. *Elephant Encyclopedia.* www.upali.ch/swim_en.html.

"Philadelphia History." www.ushistory.org/philadelphia/timeline/ 1847.htm

Philadelphia Inquirer, April 16, 1874.

A Man Invents His Killer—1867

Harry Ransom Center. "Printing Yesterday and Today." www.hrc .utexas.edu/exhibitions/education/modules/gutenberg/books/ printing/.

Hole, Robert. *A Short History of the Printing Press and of Improvements in Printing Machinery from the Time of Gutenberg up to the Present Day.* 1902.

Smithsonian Institution. "Rotary Perfecting Press." *History Wired: A Few of Our Favorite Things.* http://historywired.si.edu/object .cfm?ID=401.

"William Bullock (inventor)." http://en.wikipedia.org/wiki/ William_Bullock_(inventor).

The Autopsy of Chang and Eng—1874
Anderson, Elizabeth. "Chang and Eng Bunker: The Siamese Twins." *Phreequeshow.* http://phreeque.tripod.com/chang_ eng.html.

Chichester, Page. "A Hyphenated Life." *Blue Ridge Country,* November/December 2005. http://blueridgecountry.com/ newtwins/twins.html.

Wallace, Amy, and Irving Wallace. *The Two: The Story of the Original Siamese Twins.* New York: Simon and Schuster, 1978.

The Great Exposition—1876
Free Library of Philadelphia. *Centennial Exhibition Digital Collection.* http://libwww.library.phila.gov/CenCol/.

Garrison, Webb. *A Treasury of Pennsylvania Tales: Unusual, Interesting, and Little-Known Stories of Pennsylvania.* Nashville: Rutledge Hill Press, 1996.

McCabe, James D. *The Illustrated History of the Centennial Exhibition.* 1876. Reprint, Philadelphia: National Publishing Company, 1975.

Raatma, Lucia. *Alexander Graham Bell.* Minneapolis: Compass Point Books, 2005.

A Runaway Kid—1892
Curtis, James. *W. C. Fields: A Biography.* New York: Alfred A. Knopf, 2003.

Taylor, Robert Lewis. *W. C. Fields: His Follies and Fortunes.* Garden City, NY: Doubleday, 1949.

Mummer's Parade—1901
Dubin, Murray. *South Philadelphia: Mummers, Memories, and the Melrose Diner.* Philadelphia: Temple University Press, 1996.

Miers, Earl Schenk. *Golden Slippers: The Story of Philadelphia and Its Mummer's Parade.* Newark, DE: The Curtis Paper Company, 1966.

Philadelphia Bulletin, January 2, 1901. "Elkton Club Wins Big Mummer Prize," p. 2-B.

Philadelphia Inquirer, January 1, 1901. "How Mummer's Will March Today," p. 2-A.

———. January 2, 1901. "Merry Mummer's In Motley Garb Hold Sway In Mommoth Pagent – Edith Langdon Sees The Parade – Prize Winner's In Shooter's Parade – Clubs Compete For City Prizes," p. 2-B.

Philadelphia Public Ledger, January 2, 1901. "Masker's Carnival," p. 2-A.

A Sticky Situation—1928

Dubble Bubble Web site. www.dubblebubble.com/index.html.

"Fleer Corporation." www.fundinguniverse.com/company-histories/ Fleer-Corporation-Company-History.html.

Pipa, Brian. "The History of Chewing Gum." http://candyaddict .com/blog/2005/12/30/the-history-of-chewing-gum/.

"Walter E. Diemer." www.cbsd.org/pennsylvaniapeople/level1_ biographies/Biographies_Level1/walter_diemer_level_1.htm.

Wardlaw, Lee. *Bubblemania: The Chewy History of Bubble Gum.* New York: Aladdin Paperbacks, 1997.

Whole Pop Magazine Online. "Blibber-Blubber Double Bubble." *Chewing Gum.* www.wholepop.com/features/chewing_gum/ blibber_blubber.htm.

World Book Encyclopedia. Chicago: World Book, Inc., 1995 and 2002.

World Book Encyclopedia. Chicago: Field Enterprises, 1960.

The 1929 Athletics—1929

Dickey, Glenn. *The History of the World Series.* Briarcliff Manor, NY: Stein and Day, 1984.

James, Bill. *The Bill James Guide to Baseball Managers: From 1970 to Today.* New York: Scribner, 1997.

————. *Historical Baseball Abstract.* New York: Free Press, 2001.

Kashatus, William C. *Connie Mack's '29 Triumph: The Rise and Fall of the Philadelphia Athletics Dynasty.* Jefferson, NC: MacFarland and Company, 1999.

Monopoly, a Game of Big Money—1936
Brady, Maxine. *The Monopoly Book: Strategy and Tactics of the World's Most Popular Game.* David McKay, 1975. http://richard_wilding.tripod.com/history.htm.

Parlett, David. *The Oxford History of Board Games.* New York: Oxford University Press, 1999.

Wolfe, Burton H. "The Monopolization of Monopoly." *San Francisco Bay Guardian,* April 23, 1976.

ENIAC: The First Electronic Digital Computer—1947
Goldschmidt, Asaf, and Atsushi Akera. "John W. Mauchly and the Development of the ENIAC Computer." Penn Library Exhibitions. www.library.upenn.edu/exhibits/rbm/mauchly/jwmintro.html.

McCartney, Scott. *ENIAC: The Triumphs and Tragedies of the World's First Computer.* New York: Walker and Company, 1999.

Richey, Kevin W. "The ENIAC." February 1997. http://ei.cs.vt.edu/~history/ENIAC.Richey.HTML.

Shurkin, Joel. *Engines of the Mind: The Evolution of the Computer from Mainframes to Microprocessors.* New York: W. W. Norton, 1996.

Weik, Martin H. "The ENIAC Story." *ORDNANCE,* January–February 1961. http://ftp.arl.army.mil/~mike/comphist/eniac-story.html.

A Miracle—1949

American Catholic. "St. John Neumann." www.americancatholic.org/Features/SaintOfDay/default.asp?id=1251.

Boston Globe, June 19, 1977. "It's John Neumann," U.S. & World, p. 57.

———. June 20, 1977. "His name is now in the calendar of saints," p. 1-A.

Catholic Online. "St. John Neumann." www.catholic.org/saints/saint.php?saint_id=70.

Cullen, Sister Mary Laurena. "The Bishop Neumann Shrine in Sugar Ridge." *Roots Web.* www.rootsweb.com/~pasulliv/churches/Laurena.htm.

National Shrine of St. John Neumann. "Life of Saint John Neumann, Miracle Worker." www.stjohnneumann.org/life.html and www.salisburypa.com/life.html.

Philadelphia Inquirer, July 18, 1976. "How the Bishop finally won sainthood," p. 1-A.

———. July 23, 1976. "2 Major sculptors," p. 3-C.

———. June 19, 1977. "Today the City has a saint," p. 1-A; "Today at the Vatican, Philadelphia gains a saint," p. 10-A.

Philadelphia Inquirer Today Magazine, August 1, 1976.

American Bandstand—1957

Clark, Dick, and Richard Robinson. *Rock, Roll, and Remember.* Crowell, New York: Hoyt Press, 1976.

Goldmine Magazine, ed. *Goldmine Roots of Rock Digest.* Iola, WI: Krause Publications, 1999.

Jackson, John A. *American Bandstand: Dick Clark and the Making of a Rock 'n' Roll Empire.* New York: Oxford University Press, 1997.

Wilt's 100—1962

Chamberlain, Wilt. *A View from Above.* New York: Signet Books, 1992.

NBA's Greatest Moments. "Wilt Scores 100!" *NBA Encyclopedia.* www.nba.com/history/wilt100_moments.html.

Pomerantz, Gary M. *Wilt, 1962: The Night of 100 Points and the Dawn of a New Era.* New York: Crown, 2005.

Williams, Juan. "Remembering the Night of 100 Points." www.npr.org/templates/story/story.php?storyId=4704533

The Snowball Santa Incident—1968

AllExperts.com. *Philadelphia Eagles Encyclopedia.* http://experts .about.com/e/p/ph/Philadelphia_Eagles.htm.

Macnow, Glen, and Anthony L. Gargano. *The Great Philadelphia Fan Book.* Moorestown, NJ: Middle Atlantic Press, 2003.

Mihoces, Gary. "Santa snowball incident shrouded in myth." *USA Today,* November 27, 2003. www.usatoday.com/sports/football/nfl/eagles/2003-11-27-santa-snowballs_x.htm.

An Elusive Killer—1976

Altman, Lawrence K. "In Philadelphia 30 Years Ago, an Eruption of Illness and Fear." *New York Times,* August 1, 2006.

Huntington, Tom. "The Park Hyatt Philadelphia at the Bellevue." Primedia Publications. http://away.com/primedia/index.html.

Philadelphia Inquirer, August 3–15, 1976.

———. August 3, 1976, "Mysterious Disease Kills 16 . . .," p. 1-A.

———. August 4, 1976, "Mystery Death Toll Reaches 20," p. 1-A.

———. August 5, 1976, "3 Causes Likely for Disease," p. 1-A; "Legionnaires bury one member, pray for the next one who dies," p. 4-A.

———. August 7, 1976, ". . . Focus on Toxins," p. 1; "Fearless," pp. 1, 8.

———. August 8, 1976, "6 days, 25 deaths . . . no answers," sec. A, pp. 1, 4, 6.

———. August 9, 1976, "2 more die . . .," p. 1-A.

———. August 13, 1976, "Several agents ruled out . . .," p. 1-C.

———. August 15, 1976, "The disease hunt: . . . and Disease claims new victim," p. 1.

Thomas, Gordon, and Max Morgan-Witts. *Anatomy of an Epidemic.* Garden City, NY: Doubleday, 1982.

Million-Dollar Mania—1981

Bowden, Mark. *Finders Keepers: The Story of a Man Who Found $1 Million.* New York: Atlantic Monthly Press, 2002.

Money for Nothing. Screenplay directed by Ramón Menéndez. California: Hollywood Pictures, September 10, 1993.

INDEX

ABOUT THE AUTHOR

Scott Brucc is a professional comedian who performs in every available venue including television, radio, stage, colleges, cruise ships, and comedy clubs. He was the host of *The Pennsylvania Game,* a long-running television trivia show airing on PBS. With Fran Capo, he is the co-author of *It Happened in Pennsylvania.* He resides in the Pocono Mountains with his wife, Anne, and their two children, Nicholas and Chloe.